AD PEVENE SI...

The Life and Times of
WILLIAM I

The Life and Times of
WILLIAM I

Maurice Ashley

Introduction by Antonia Fraser

BCA
LONDON · NEW YORK · SYDNEY · TORONTO

Series designed by Paul Watkins
Layout by Sheila Sherwin

Filmset by Keyspools Limited, Golborne, Lancs
Printed in Great Britain by
Butler & Tanner Ltd, Frome and London

Contents

Acknowledgments

Photographs and illustrations were supplied or are reproduced by kind permission of the following: Photo Alfa: 72; Bibliothèque Nationale, Paris: 64, 130–1; Bodleian Library: 57, 114 (*above*), 158; British Museum: 2, 3, 19, 22, 48, 49, 58, 65, 93, 95, 97, 102, 103, 104, *109* (*above*), 114 (*below*), 119, 134–5, 152, 153, 154, 163, 166, 168–9, 171, 172–3, 175, *180*, 182–3, 185, 189 (*below*), *192*, 195, 200, 204 (*above*), 205, 208, 214, 215; British Printing Corporation: *109* (*below*); Cambridge University Library: *109* (*below*); J. Allan Cash: 87, 89, 158, 161; Dean and Chapter of Chichester Cathedral: 210 (*below*); Master and Fellows of Corpus Christi College, Cambridge: 186–7; Courtauld Institute: 117 (*above*), 211 (*below left*)©Professor G. Zarnecki; Dean and Chapter of Durham Cathedral: 204 (*below*); Department of the Environment: 83 (*below*); Giraudon: 54; Glasgow Art Gallery and Museum, Burrell Collection: 137; Guildhall Museum: 210 (*above*); Robert Harding: 121; Michael Holford: *14–15*, *34–5*, *46–7*; A.F.Kersting: 76–7, 211 (*below right*); Künsthistorisches Museum, Vienna: 122; Mansell Collection: 56; Meridian Airmaps: 38; National Museum, Stockholm: *177* (*above*); Pierpont Morgan Library: *100*; Popperfoto: 70, 126 (*right*), 127 (*above*) photo by Donald McLeish, 127 (*below*); Public Record Office: 106–7, 150; Royal Commission on Historical Monuments (Crown Copyright): 33, 82, 86, 90, 116 (*below left*, 126 (*left*), 138, 164–5; Royal Commission on Historical Monuments (© Batsford): 83 (*above*), 116 (*above*), 116 (*below right*); Royal Commission on Historical Monuments (© Rev. M.Ridgway): 211 (*right*); Scala: *177* (*below*), *189* (*above*); Science Museum: 13; Edwin Smith: 117 (*below*), 212 (*below*); Victoria and Albert Museum: 10–11, 12–13, 16, 24, 27, 28–9, 30–1, 36, 40–1, 42, 44–5, 50–1, 62–3, 98–9, 101, 110, 111, *112*, 132–3, 139, 142–3, 145, 146, 148, 149, 191, 198; Roger-Viollet: 55, 71, 73, 124, 178, 179.

Numbers in italic indicate colour illustrations.

Picture research by Jane Dorner.

Maps drawn by Design Practitioners Limited.

Introduction

For better or for worse – and the argument still rages after nine hundred years – King William I changed the face of English history in a way no sovereign before or since can claim to have done. 1066, the best known date in English history because it signifies the conquest of Anglo-Saxon England at the hands of the Normans, for once has a justified eminence in the popular imagination. What was he like, then, the man who presided over and directed this profound change-over in so many of our customs, laws and institutions? The character of the Conqueror would be worthy of study for his military and administrative importance alone: while in our own age of the European Common Market, with another very different type of Continental link being forged, and the value of separate national cultures and civilisations once more called into question, he gains an additional and special interest.

Against the background of the stirring events of William's sixty-year-long life, and twenty-year rule in England, Maurice Ashley paints a rounded and credible picture of a man who began life very much as a warrior, and who himself was to say with regret on his death-bed: 'I was bred to arms since my childhood, and am stained with the rivers of blood that I have shed.' Dr Ashley's own verdict is not so severe: he finds William harsh but not tyrannical; brave and diplomatic – by no means a common combination; an administrator rather than a law-giver, and a master of propaganda, of which the creation of the Bayeux Tapestry was a prime example; imbued with what would later be called Puritan morality, and therefore in sympathy with the Norman Archbishop Lanfranc's enthusiasm for the celibacy of the clergy (in contrast to the Anglo-Saxon church customs); above all spurred on to vigour by the stain of his illegitimate birth, which led his own age to call him William the Bastard, where we have admiringly named him William the Conqueror.

But, of course, essential to an understanding of the King's life are the complicated economic and social trends of his time. Dr Ashley threads his way with exemplary care through the maze of scholarship and historical controversy which surrounds all three civilisations with which William had contact: the Anglo-Saxon society he encountered on his arrival in England; the Norman culture of his own homeland; and the hybrid civilisation which he himself helped to create in England after the Conquest. Such knotty problems as the history of jury service, the 'Normanisation' of the English Church, and that ultimate bone of contention, 'feudalism' itself, are all considered in their place. As to the ultimate tragedy or triumph of the Conquest itself for England, this is a vexed topic indeed: on the one hand, an England woven into the cultural mainstream of Europe through Norman middlemen; on the other hand, an English peasantry whose status was undeniably lowered as the dominating Norman castles began to rise across the land. At least, every reader will be able to make up his own mind on the evidence here lucidly presented by Dr Ashley.

Antonia Fraser

Preface

IN THIS EPITOME of King William I's life and times I have been fortunate in being able to draw upon the large number of books on the subject which were published during the ten years surrounding the 900th anniversary of the Norman Conquest in 1066. My obligations to the writings of such distinguished scholars as Frank Barlow, David C. Douglas and H. R. Loyn will be obvious. Details are given in the select bibliography at the end of the book. I should also like to pay my small tribute to the memory of the late R. V. Lennard, who was one of my tutors at Oxford, and of the late Sir Frank Stenton, whom I served for a time when I was young as a temporary assistant lecturer in modern history at the University of Reading. I have to thank my friend Patrick Moore for telling me about Halley's Comet. But my debt to Frank Barlow is outstanding. I found his recent biography of Edward the Confessor incredibly stimulating and I am also grateful to him for introducing me to Dr David Bates of University College, Cardiff, who has kindly checked the facts in my book; the opinions, right or wrong, are my own.

MAURICE ASHLEY

1 The Year 1066

On MONDAY, 24 APRIL 1066 what was later to be known as Halley's Comet became visible in the path of the Sun. Comets, made up of small particles and tenuous gas, and consisting of a body with little mass and a distinctive tail, move round the Sun in elliptical orbits and can occasionally be seen from the earth for periods of weeks on end. Halley's Comet was last observed in 1910 and will be visible again in 1986. It was no wonder that when it was perceived just after Easter in 1066, it caused a sensation everywhere. 'Men looked to the sky', wrote Freeman, 'and there they saw such a token in the heavens as no man had ever seen before. Not only over all England but, as men deemed, over much of the world, the sky was ablaze with a mighty mass of flame, which no man doubted was sent to kindle a fire upon earth.' It did indeed portend extraordinary

PREVIOUS PAGES A scene from the Bayeux Tapestry showing the onslaught of Norman cavalry during the Battle of Hastings.

RIGHT An astrologer tells King Harold of an omen of misfortune, a strange star with a fiery tail which was really Halley's Comet. On the left, people are gazing in awe at the Comet in the upper border. In the lower border, ghostly ships are crossing the sea.

A photograph of Halley's Comet, last visible in 1910. The Comet can be seen from the earth at intervals of about seventy-five years.

UBI HAROLD ·SAC

VVIL

Harold, standing with
one hand upon an altar
and the other on a chest
of sacred relics, swears
allegiance to Duke William
at the castle of Bayeux;
a scene from the Bayeux
Tapestry.

RAMENTVM:FECIT:⁖ hICh

EL MO DVCI:⁖

events: for 1066 is one of the really crucial years in English history.

The ruler of England was then King Harold II (or Harold Godwineson), formerly the Earl of Wessex, that part of southern England in which Alfred the Great had begun to fashion a united Anglo-Saxon realm. Harold was a man in the prime of his life, with profound strength of character and magnanimity, who had won a reputation as a soldier both at home and abroad. He had travelled widely. His mother was a Scandinavian princess and his sister, Edith, had been married to his predecessor, King Edward the Confessor. Edward, who was childless, nominated Harold his successor as he lay dying on 5 January, and the next day his choice was confirmed – apparently unanimously – by the group of magnates meeting in what was known as the Witanegemot, which was summoned by the king three times a year to give him advice. The members of the Witanegemot happened to be in London at the end of 1065, at the moment when Westminster Abbey, to the building of which Edward the Confessor had devoted much of the last years of his life, was due to be consecrated and in which Edward himself was to be buried.

English monarchs were not chosen simply by primogeniture or heredity. Almost any great nobleman who had some royal blood in his veins (as Harold had) might stake his claim. At the beginning of 1066, a plethora of candidates was available. One was Harold Hardrada, King of Norway, who believed that the throne of England had been promised to his father, King Magnus, by King Harthacnut, Edward the Confessor's immediate predecessor; another was Prince Edgar ('the Atheling'), grandson of Edmund Ironside, who had been chosen King of England and who could trace his ancestry directly from Alfred the Great: but Edgar was still a youth without strong adherents. A third candidate was Duke William II of Normandy, whose antecedence was somewhat doubtful as he was himself illegitimate and his only relationship to the early English kings was that he was the great-nephew of Queen Emma, mother by her first husband of Edward the Confessor. William was therefore Edward the Confessor's second cousin once removed. But Duke William asserted that he had been promised the succession by Edward the Confessor himself in 1051 and that Harold II, when

17

PREVIOUS PAGES The death of Edward the Confessor from the Bayeux Tapestry. In the scene above, he is lying on his deathbed in an upper room of the Palace in Westminster, speaking his last words to his wife, Queen Edith, while a priest and attendants minister to him. Below, his body is laid out in state in the Great Hall.

he was still Earl of Wessex and had visited Normandy in 1064, had sworn a solemn oath to uphold the Duke's right to succeed to the English throne. William insisted that Harold was a usurper and at once prepared for an invasion of England.

Thus, from the outset of his reign, Harold was confronted with threats from all sides. Harold Hardrada had the support of Harold Godwineson's own brother Tostig, and the King of the Scots, while William not only received the approbation of his overlord, the youthful King Philip of France, but also obtained a judgment in his favour from Pope Alexander II, at whose Court Harold's case was not presented. So, when it came to the battle which Duke William had to fight against Harold II to secure the English crown, he was able to wave a papal banner and to wear consecrated relics round his neck.

William was still under forty when he invaded England, but he was an extremely experienced ruler, administrator and commander, having been for over twenty years in full charge of his duchy, the title to which he inherited in a direct line from Rollo or Rolf the Viking, a Norwegian adventurer who had established his Scandinavian followers in northern France about 918. William had fought victoriously against his neighbours, the Count of Anjou and Maine and the Duke of Brittany. He had also inflicted humiliation on his first overlord, King Henry I of France (who was succeeded by his son, Philip I, in 1049). For years Normandy had been relatively peaceful and William could safely leave it under the care of his Duchess when he invaded England. He collected a motley horde of nobles, knights and mercenaries not only from his own duchy but from all over France. The task he had set himself was by no means an impossible one. England was a small island which had often been successfully invaded, first by the Romans, then by the Anglo-Saxons, the Vikings and the Danes. It possessed many excellent harbours; the Channel between Normandy and southern England was not wide; and no regular English navy existed. Even if William could not snatch the crown, he might at least extract valuable concessions by treaty once he secured a victory over the English.

But Harold II might reasonably hope to repress all the menaces to his throne. Two influential earls, Edwin of Mercia and Morcar of Northumbria, who were brothers, had acknowl-

Harold Godwineson, the last Saxon King of England.

edged him as their King and he had married their sister, the widow of Gruffydd, the King of Wales. He too had succeeded to dominion over a placid and prosperous land. The idea which used to prevail that Edward the Confessor was a kind of holy imbecile has long been abandoned by historians. It is true that he did not much care for either his mother or his wife (both of whom he punished by confiscating their property) and that he had no children. But he proved himself a skilful statesman and warded off political threats both at home (for example, in Wales and the north) and from overseas. When he died a native poet wrote of him:

> Here in the world he dwelt for a time
> In royal majesty, sagacious in counsel;
> A gracious ruler for twenty-four years
> And a half, he dispensed bounties.
> Ruler of warriors, son of Ethelred,
> Greatly distinguished, he ruled Welsh,
> Scots and Britons too,
> Angles and Saxons, his eager soldiers.

So it was neither internal disturbances nor lack of resources that handicapped Harold, but only the coming of rivals from abroad who disputed his title and hoped to reap profits before he could establish himself firmly as the new king.

Before William the Conqueror's campaign in England during 1066 is described, let us consider more precisely the nature of William's claim to succeed Edward the Confessor on the English throne. First, it must be said that the fact that Edward's mother, Queen Emma, was also the great-aunt of William should not be taken too seriously. Succession to the throne, as has already been noted, had little to do with complicated blood relationships. Indeed, Queen Emma herself (who died in 1052) is known to have favoured the succession not of William but of Harold Hardrada of Norway. Although she had given birth to Edward the Confessor by her first husband, Ethelred 'the Unready', she always preferred her sons by her second husband, King Canute, whose father had been King of Denmark and who himself had conquered Norway. Secondly, it must be remembered that the story of William's claims is derived entirely from Norman chroniclers and even these are not independent. William of Poitiers, who was a chaplain of William the Conqueror and Archdeacon of Lisieux in Normandy, began his panegyric about 1072 and based it partly on the writings of an earlier Norman historian, William of Jumièges, and a poem about the Battle of Hastings. The Bayeux Tapestry, a stitchwork commissioned by Bishop Odo of Bayeux, William's half-brother, about twelve years after 1066, and which has been relied upon by several of William's biographers as a relatively impartial description of events, mainly followed the narrative of William of Poitiers. Thirdly, English medieval experts – even those who have been writing during the past thirty years – are by no means in agreement about what exactly happened.

The story begins before Edward the Confessor became King of England, because he was brought up in Normandy and thus, it is assumed, felt he owed a debt to the Normans. His favouritism towards Normans and other Frenchmen has been exaggerated, but he certainly appointed Robert of Jumièges, a Norman, as his Archbishop of Canterbury and listened to his advice. In 1051, the year in which Robert of Jumièges was promoted, Edward received a visit from Count Eustace of Boulogne, his French brother-in-law. Either on his way to

King Canute and his wife,
Emma of Normandy,
presenting a charter to the
Church. Canute, King of
Denmark, was accepted by
the English as King when
Edmund Ironside died.
Queen Emma was the
mother of Edward the
Confessor by her first
husband, and a great-aunt
of Duke William.

King Edward the
Confessor, who spent his
youth in exile in
Normandy. During his
reign Norman influences at
Court were considerable,
though the Normans gave
him little support in his
struggle against the
powerful Godwin family.

England or on his way back, Eustace's men were involved in an affray with the citizens of Dover, and some twenty were killed there. Edward ordered Godwin, his father-in-law, who was then Earl of Wessex and whose territory included Dover, to punish the citizens of the port. Godwin refused, either because he did not see why he should alienate his own vassals or because he thought that the French were to blame for the incident. Edward, who was no weakling, called up an army to confront Godwin's men and commanded Godwin to appear before a meeting of the Witanegemot at Gloucester. When Godwin refused to attend, Edward sent him into exile. Godwin, who did not want to engage in a drawn-out civil war, accepted his exile, along with his sons, the second of whom was Harold, the future king of England.

Edward realised that Godwin, who was the most powerful earl in the kingdom, was unlikely voluntarily to remain in exile for long. The King therefore looked round for help and it was not unnatural for him to turn to Duke William, who had by then established himself as a strong ruler. Therefore, according to the narrative of William of Jumièges, Edward dispatched his new Archbishop, who was in any case going to Rome to receive the *pallium* (or cloak of honour) from the Pope, with a message to the effect that the throne of England was to be bequeathed to the Duke of Normandy. One English chronicler states that William himself came to England, probably about Christmas 1051; why he came is not known: the suggestion that it was to pay a courtesy visit to his great-aunt who was dying seems a trifle implausible. It is, however, likely that Edward wanted to conclude a treaty of friendship with the Duke of Normandy, especially after he had quarrelled with Godwin and exiled him and had also sent Godwin's daughter, his own wife, into a nunnery. Yet that at this stage in his reign (he was to live for another fifteen years) Edward named William as his heir is hard to credit. It is true that the King might have held out vague promises to secure the Duke's friendship. As it was, when Godwin and his sons carried through a counter-revolution in 1052, William gave Edward no help. The English King was obliged to rid himself of most of his Norman entourage and to replace Robert of Jumièges as Archbishop of Canterbury with an Englishman, Stigand, Bishop of Winchester. Godwin

himself died a year afterwards; but for the remainder of Edward's reign Godwin's second son, Harold, Earl of Wessex became one of the King's principal counsellors and directed military operations on Edward's behalf along the Welsh border.

In the summer of 1064, Harold visited Normandy and was honourably entertained at Duke William's Court in Rouen. Harold had embarked at Bosham, a family estate in Sussex, not an obvious point of departure if his first intention was to sail to Normandy. Three conjectures about Harold's voyage have been made: one is that he was merely going fishing; the second is that he had been ordered by King Edward to visit William so as to secure the release of two hostages whom the King had given to William in 1051, Wulfnoth, one of Harold's numerous brothers, and Hakon, one of his many nephews. The third explanation, which is supported by all the Norman sources and not contradicted by any English authority (that is to say in effect the *Anglo-Saxon Chronicle*), is that Edward sent Harold to confirm by oath the bequest of the throne which the King is alleged to have made to William in 1051.

What is not in doubt is that the wind blew Harold's ships towards Ponthieu, which lay just to the east of Normandy, and Harold was obliged to land there. He was then imprisoned or at least threatened with imprisonment by Count Guy of Ponthieu in order that he might obtain a ransom. Hearing about this, William at once sent messengers to Guy, who was his vassal, ordering the release of Harold immediately on penalty of war. Harold was thereupon freed and set out for Normandy; William met the Earl *en route* and brought him to his palace at Rouen. William of Poitiers attributes to the Duke a speech which he delivered on the eve of the Battle of Hastings:

> ... finally Edward sent Harold himself to Normandy so that he could swear to me in my presence what his father [Godwin] and Earls Leofric and Siward [Earls of Mercia and Northumbria] had sworn to me here in my absence. On the journey Harold incurred the danger of being taken prisoner, from which, using force and diplomacy, I rescued him. Through his own hands he made himself my vassal and with his own hand he gave me a firm pledge concerning the kingdom of England.

The Bayeux Tapestry pictures Harold taking an oath of allegiance with both hands placed upon holy shrines. But the

OPPOSITE Harold and his friends entering a church at Bosham to pray for a safe voyage, before setting out on their mission to Normandy in the summer of 1064.

OVERLEAF
An escaped Englishman tells Duke William in his castle at Rouen that Harold has been taken prisoner by William's vassal, Count Guy of Ponthieu.

Norman authorities do not agree whether the oath was given at Rouen, Bayeux or Bonneville-sur-Touques near Lisieux. Afterwards, William took his guest with him on a campaign in Brittany during which Harold distinguished himself. William then knighted Harold and released his nephew Hakon, who had been a hostage.

The question remains how far the story told by William of Poitiers is to be trusted. Is it likely that the chief men of England swore a corporeal oath to the young Duke that they would accept him as Edward's successor years before Edward died? Was Harold really sent over by Edward? What was the nature of Harold's sacred undertaking? Did he in fact promise to uphold William's claim to the throne of England and to become his representative (*vicarius*) there or did he simply, as one modern historian has argued, swear 'to observe the long-standing treaty of amity between the King and the Duke and in return was granted the release of his nephew'? Did he perhaps pledge himself to marry William's eldest daughter, Agatha? A final alternative is that the oath was extracted by force, just as the Normans alleged that Edward the Confessor's death-bed bequest of the throne to Harold was given under pressure.

During the following year, a rebellion broke out in Northumbria against its earl, who was then one of Harold's brothers, Tostig by name. Tostig was reputedly Edward the Confessor's favourite, and Harold exerted himself to arrange a compromise between his brother and his brother's vassals. In this he was unsuccessful. The Northumbrians insisted on the appointment of Morcar, the brother of Earl Edwin of Mercia, in Tostig's place. Thus it was obvious to Duke William that the power of the House of Godwin had been seriously weakened. That may well have been the determining factor which induced him to prepare for an invasion of England in the following year. It used to be urged that the Norman Conquest was neither Norman nor a conquest, first because others than Normans served in William's expeditionary army and secondly because William claimed merely to be enforcing his unquestionable hereditary right to succeed to the throne. But that is sheer paradox. William and his Normans organised the expedition, while the story that Edward the Confessor bequeathed his throne to William in 1051 and that Harold, Earl of Wessex

ABOVE On the left, Harold is offered
the crown of England in succession
to Edward the Confessor. On the right,
he is shown seated on the throne,
crowned and holding the orb and
sceptre, the symbols of monarchy.
Beside him, Archbishop Stigand
proclaims the new King to the people.

SIDET:hAROLD
GLORVM:
STIGANT
ARChiEPS

Building the fleet for the invasion of England: on the left, men are felling trees for timber; on the right, craftsmen are making the boats, using axes, adzes and other tools.

confirmed the bequest in 1064, depends purely on Norman propagandists and is extremely doubtful.

But as soon as he became King of England, Harold recognised that his country was likely to be invaded both in the south and in the north. He first rode up to unruly Northumbria and established his headquarters at York. There he was helped by the Archbishop of York, while his marriage to the sister of Morcar, Earl of Northumbria, strengthened his position. He returned to Westminster in time for Easter and for a view of 'the long-haired star' which appeared in the sky. The first threat to his supremacy came from his rebellious brother Tostig, who blamed Harold rather unfairly for the loss of his earldom. In

April, Tostig managed to collect money and provisions in the Isle of Wight and in Sandwich, but disappeared as soon as he learned that the King was on his way south; so instead of ravaging the southern coasts, Tostig sailed north and joined Malcolm III, the King of Scots.

Tostig's withdrawal gave Harold some reason for optimism, but he still feared an invasion from Normandy. Therefore he moved his headquarters to the south of England, accompanied by his housecarls, trained and disciplined knights firmly attached to the royal service; he called up the militia, or Anglo-Saxon 'fyrd'; and he stationed a large fleet off the Isle of Wight. For four months Harold remained in the south ready to repel an invasion. But when September came and nothing had happened, Harold dismissed his militia – for it was high time to gather in the harvest – and withdrew his fleet to London, losing many of his ships in the process.

During the spring and summer, William of Normandy had been far from idle. But he needed first to persuade the hesitant Norman aristocracy to agree to the invasion of England; only the impetuous favoured the enterprise, while others thought that 'a handful of Normans could not conquer a huge multitude of Englishmen'; secondly, transports had to be built to carry his army, including cavalry, across the Channel; thirdly, he set about recruiting mercenaries wherever he could find them; and lastly, he needed to employ all his diplomacy to win the moral support of the Pope and Emperor, the two highest dignitaries in Europe. Moreover, the winds blowing from the north were unpropitious for a crossing. There may have been an unfortunate first attempt (as when William, Prince of Orange, invaded England in 1688), for, according to William of Poitiers, the Norman Duke concealed as best he could 'the deaths of those who were engulfed by the waves'. But on learning of the break-up of the English defences in the south of England, William ordered the removal of the fleet from the south of the River Dives to St Valéry in the mouth of the Somme, whence the passage across the Channel was shorter. After appropriate prayers had been made to St Valéry, the wind changed and the invasion fleet set out on the night of 27 September 1066. William himself was carried upon the fastest ship, unsuitably named *Mora* (which in Latin means delay), donated by his Duchess.

Meanwhile Harold was far away in the north of England. In the middle of September, King Harold Hardrada of Norway had arrived with three hundred ships off the mouth of the Tyne; here he was joined by Harold's brother Tostig and reinforcements from Scotland. On 18 September the combined forces entered the Humber and landed at Riccall on the Yorkshire Ouse, ten miles from York. As they approached the city, they were confronted by an army commanded by the brother Earls of Northumbria and Mercia at Gate Fulford just south of the city. The battle on 20 September was long and bloody, but Hardrada was victorious and was able to occupy York. King

ABOVE The medieval city walls of York. The city
was taken by Harold Hardrada, King of Norway,
in September 1066, but was won back a few weeks
later by King Harold of England after the Norwegians
had been defeated at the Battle of Stamford Bridge.

OVERLEAF The invasion
fleet crossing the
English Channel, the
ships tightly packed with
men and horses.

NAVIGIO:

MARE

Harold can hardly have heard the news of the northern invasion more than a couple of days before the Battle of Gate Fulford. He immediately began a forced march up the old Roman road through York, where he expected the enemy to be, and faced the invaders at Stamford Bridge, on the River Derwent, seven miles east of York. The Norwegians were surprised by the speed of Harold's coming. After a fierce battle on 25 September, they were utterly defeated and Harold Hardrada and Tostig were killed; the English King gave quarter to Olaf, the son of the dead Norwegian King, who promised to maintain peace and friendship henceforward with the English people. But on 1 October, King Harold learned what he had long dreaded: William of Normandy had disembarked without opposition at Pevensey in Sussex.

William had organised his expedition in precise detail. The loading and unloading of the horses on the sailing ships of those days must alone have been a serious problem. But William was

36

also aided by luck. The wind changed at a wonderfully convenient time so that he was able to reach England while King Harold was still away in the north. After surveying the area around Pevensey, William decided to move his army to Hastings, which was a better port in a more defensible area, and there he erected a castle or at any rate fortifications. As an almost contemporary French poet apostrophised him:

> Fearing to lose the ships,
> You surrounded them with earthworks,
> And guarded the shores.
> Which had stood formerly,
> And set guardians to hold them.
> Having gained control,
> Though over no great space,
> Your people attacked the region,
> Laid it waste, and burnt it
> With fire. Small wonder, the foolish folk
> Denied that you were king!
> Therefore they perished justly
> And went to destruction.

Duke William's aim was to keep close touch with his ships because he knew that he had a severe struggle ahead of him and might even be thrust back to the sea. Robert fitz Wimarch, a nobleman of Norman origin, sent a message to the Duke warning him that the victorious Harold was leading 'a large and very strong army', compared with which the Normans were 'despicable dogs'. Harold in fact covered the distance of two hundred and fifty miles from York to Hastings in fewer than thirteen days, and that included a halt of four or five days in London to enlist recruits. He can have been accompanied from York by only his mounted housecarls. His infantry or militiamen were desperately scraped together from the southern shires, for many of the best fighting men in England had been left behind in the north.

Harold clearly hoped to surprise William by the swiftness of his coming, as he had surprised Harold Hardrada near York. But William was aware of Harold's imminent approach and even before his enemy's arrival on the evening of 13 October had set up an advanced post on Telham Hill to the north of Hastings that guarded the entry into what was then a natural

The Norman army landing at Pevensey in Sussex. There was no resistance to the landing since King Harold was in the north of England dealing with the Norwegian invaders.

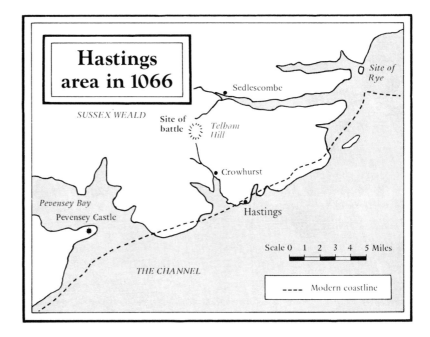

Hastings area in 1066

SUSSEX WEALD

Sedlescombe

Site of Rye

Site of battle

Telham Hill

Crowhurst

Pevensey Bay

Pevensey Castle

Hastings

Scale 0 1 2 3 4 5 Miles

THE CHANNEL

- - - - Modern coastline

BELOW An aerial view of the battlefield at Hastings.

peninsula, formed by tidal waters on each side, which today are nothing but streams. Nevertheless, Harold had once again achieved a strategic surprise because, owing to an all-night advance with his mounted men, he had been able to pour troops out of the Sussex Weald and concentrate them on a lonely and hilly stretch of land marked only by a 'grey apple tree'. There the English prepared to fight the invaders on a six-hundred-yard front, fully protected on each flank by marshy streams. When the news of Harold's taking up this key position, which blocked the road to London, became known to William early in the morning of 14 October, some of the Duke's advanced guard were out foraging and those in the camp upon Telham Hill were unarmed.

Now both sides made ready for battle. King Harold erected his two standards, the Dragon of Wessex and a banner of the Fighting Man, in the left centre of his front, which was later to become the site of the high altar of Battle Abbey. William, for his part, in spite of the tactical disadvantages – for a valley lay between Telham Hill and Harold's line and therefore the Duke and his men had to transverse it and then attack uphill – determined to seize the initiative. Indeed, William may have tried vainly to prevent Harold from drawing up his troops upon the hill after they had emerged from the forest. At any rate, William must immediately have called up his main body of knights from Hastings with a view to dislodging the English from their well-chosen ground.

William divided his soldiers into three groups: on the left, the Bretons; on the right, a mixed force of knights and mercenaries under Count Eustace of Boulogne; and in the centre, the main Norman body with the Duke himself at its head. Harold had arranged his men as a shield wall; they were armed mostly with javelins and two-handed axes. His aim was to break the Norman charge uphill and then to counter-attack. Neither commander had any intention of fighting a purely defensive battle.

It is pretty certain that the armies each contained not more than seven thousand men. In view of the nature of the country and the narrow frontage, Harold dismounted his housecarls, who formed the core of his army; but he possessed few archers. William had a cavalry force, mounted upon the horses he had shipped over from Normandy, and more archers than the

The Battle of Hastings:
Harold's housecarls,
having formed a
shieldwall, resist the
onslaught of the
Norman troops.

English. On the whole, his army was the more experienced. But there was little difference in the weapons or even the tactics of the two armies. It is true that the Normans were able to essay a cavalry charge, but one must not think of that in terms of the cavalry charges under Marlborough and Villars or even of Rupert and Cromwell. William's horsemen fought with their javelins or swords and could easily be turned back or dismounted by the massed English. William had three horses killed under him during the battle. The knights on both sides wore much the same equipment, consisting of a knee-length

'birnie' or coat of chain armour and a helmet with a nosepiece.

The battle began at about nine in the morning of 14 October when William sent forward his infantry to attack the English position. Then a hail of arrows and bolts from crossbows followed; and finally his mounted men went in with their swords. Hand-to-hand fighting developed, and it is likely that at this stage of the battle two of Harold's brothers who fought alongside him were killed. But all these attacks by the Normans were thrust back and they were compelled to retreat. It looked as if the English had won the day. If Harold had been able to counter-attack at this moment, it might have been so, but his men were over-confident in the impregnability of their shield wall. 'Some were moved by love for Harold,' admitted William of Poitiers, 'and all were inspired by love of their country which they desired, however unjustly, to defend against foreigners.' It was Duke William himself who turned the scales against the English. A rumour had spread that he had been killed, so he removed his helmet to reassure his followers that he was still alive and thus stopped any panic. Throughout, William was in control of the battle and he now resolved upon a co-ordinated assault by all his forces, cavalry, light infantry and archers. It is also related that feigned retreats were made by his men to tempt the English out of their positions: that is doubtful, for it was a difficult manœuvre to execute except with highly-trained men. After what may have been the third attack, King Harold himself was killed, struck down by a mounted knight with his sword. (The story that he was killed by an arrow landing in his eye is one of the well-worn legends of British history, but is based upon a misunderstanding of the Bayeux Tapestry depicting the battle.) After the loss of their monarch, the English took flight. The battle had gone on all day and as darkness fell William called off the pursuit. He encamped on the site of the battle. Harold's body was found and buried unconsecrated upon a cliff above the seashore.

After his victory, William hoped for a general submission. The remaining English leaders, the Earls Morcar and Edwin and the two Archbishops, had considered recognising the boy Edgar as the new King. They gathered in London to discuss the matter, but nothing was agreed and the two Earls left the south of England. William proceeded cautiously; he wanted to avoid

Harold's brothers, Leofwyn and Gyrth, are killed by Norman knights during the battle.

43

a full-scale assault on London. First, he compelled Dover to surrender to him, thus keeping open the best Channel crossing, and then he took Canterbury, the capital of Kent; he encamped near there for four weeks where he was taken ill. Edith, the widow of Edward the Confessor and sister of Harold II, who was at Winchester, where the English treasure was kept, hastened to capitulate under threat of siege. Thus the whole of south-east England was in the conqueror's hands. William first moved towards London Bridge and beat off an attack there. Then he set fire to Southwark and turned back through

A group of Saxon soldiers, isolated on a hillock, are attacked by the Norman cavalry.

Hampshire into Berkshire, laying waste the country as he went. Finally he crossed the river near Wallingford and camped at Berkhampstead where, according to the *Anglo-Saxon Chronicle*:

> ... he was met by Bishop Aldred [the Archbishop of York], Prince Edgar, Earl Edwin, Earl Morcar and all the best men from London, who submitted from force of circumstances, but only when the depredation was complete. . . . They gave him hostages and swore oaths of fealty, and he promised to be a gracious lord to them.

But the monkish chronicler thought that they would have been wiser to surrender earlier.

On the left, Harold is
killed, having been
struck by a rider with a
sword; on the right, the
last stages of battle.
After the death of
their King, the English
were disheartened and fled
from the battlefield.

46

ona
villi
nor
nie.

NORMAN
villus ut
londonia
adiens ir
magna e
ultacōne
clero † ꝑ
suscept̃ e
ab omni
rex aꞇla
tus. dñic

natiuitatis die ab aldredo ebor archiepo ꞇ
ni suscepit diadema. Timuit. n̄. hoc inu
ꝯsecratōis a stigando cant̃ archiepo suscı̷
eo ꝙ nō legittime occupauit ille excellentia
dignitatis. licz de iure antiq̃ ad illā eccan
illa sollempnitas spectare coplet̃. verñ h̷

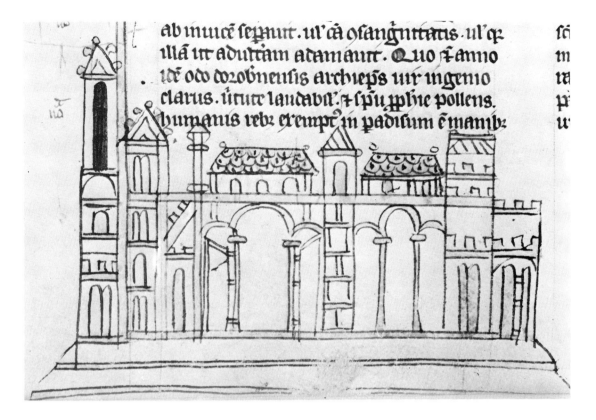

It was arranged that William should be crowned the King of the English 'by the grant of God' in Westminster Abbey on Christmas Day. He was anointed there with holy oil by the archbishops or other bishops. Thus it was an early example of divine, but not hereditary right. The congregation was asked in English to acknowledge their new King. When the mounted guard outside heard the shouting, they thought that William had been attacked and promptly set fire to the surrounding buildings. No shouts, oaths or ceremonies, however, could conceal the fact that England was a vanquished country. William gave orders that a fortress should be built to overawe the capital, which subsequently became the Tower of London. Within three months of his coronation, William thought that it was safe and necessary for him to return to Normandy, which he had ruled since his youth.

ABOVE Westminster Abbey, where William I was crowned on Christmas Day, 1066. He was the first King of England to be crowned in the Abbey.

OPPOSITE The coronation of William from a thirteenth-century manuscript.

2
The Duke
of
Normandy
1028-66

WILLIAM HAD NOT BEGUN his reign as Duke of Normandy under auspicious circumstances. It is true that his ancestors had been firmly established there for over a hundred years when he was born, probably in the autumn of 1028. Charles III, King of the Franks, known as 'the Simple', had allowed Rolf the Viking to colonise a stretch of northern France with his Norwegians. Here they mixed with the local inhabitants, and Rolf had become a Christian. By the end of the tenth century, most Normans spoke French, and the Scandinavian influences were not overwhelming. Rolf and his first two successors as rulers had seemingly been known as Counts; William's great-grandfather, Richard I, was the first to assume the title of duke. The dynasty had extended its territories, which were efficiently governed by *comtes* (counts) and *vicomtes* (viscounts). But as William himself was illegitimate and succeeded to the throne when he was only seven years old, it was obvious that political chaos was likely to arise, as it invariably did during a medieval minority.

The rulers of Normandy were prolific and bastardy had never been a bar to inheritance. Nevertheless, it engendered obloquy and William was usually known to his contemporaries as William the Bastard rather than William the Conqueror. His father, Duke Robert I, had experienced difficulties with Robert, Archbishop of Rouen and Count of Evreux, who was his uncle, and also with his cousin Alan III, the Count of neighbouring Brittany. But, in due course, everybody was reconciled and Robert I of Normandy was on friendly terms with his overlord, King Henry I of France (Richard I had accepted that he was a vassal of the French King, Hugh Capet).

Just before or after he came to the throne, Duke Robert I formed a liaison with Herleve – sometimes called Arlette – the daughter of a tanner in Falaise; they were both about seventeen at the time. Arlette gave birth to William the Bastard and to a daughter, Adelaide. Sexual relations in reality were rarely as they have been romantically pictured by Christian writers about the Middle Ages – that is to say maritally pure. Archbishop Robert had three children by his mistress, and most Norman dukes had concubines and illegitimate children. Robert was apparently betrothed to a sister of King Canute of Denmark and in due course he found a husband for Arlette in one of his

PREVIOUS PAGES A scene from the Bayeux Tapestry showing Duke William, after his arrival in England, holding a council of war with his two half-brothers, Bishop Odo, on the left, and Count Robert of Mortain, on the right.

vassals, a viscount by whom she had two sons, one of whom was the future Bishop of Bayeux. Thus there could be no doubt at all about William's bastardy. It is presumed that during his early childhood he was looked after by his mother in Falaise. But in 1034, Duke Robert made two surprising resolutions: first, he announced that he was going on a pilgrimage to Jerusalem; secondly, before he left, he summoned the Norman magnates, headed by Archbishop Robert of Rouen, and persuaded them to recognise William as his son and heir. When in July 1035 Robert I died suddenly on his way back from Jerusalem, William became Duke. At first, the accession of a child was accepted without mishap. His great-uncle looked after him and the government, instead of claiming the succession, as he might reasonably have done, for himself or his own children, while King Henry I of France, as the overlord of the Dukes of Normandy, had given his consent to William's claim to the throne and in due course the boy was sent to the King to perform homage.

But in March 1037, Archbishop Robert died and chaos supervened. Two of William's uncles stirred up trouble for him. Professor Douglas writes that 'William's household was in fact becoming a shambles.' Fortunately for him, most of the protagonists in this period of anarchy, which lasted for about ten years, were killed or conveniently died. In fact King Henry I of France, although he was not above prising pickings out of the anarchy, such as a castle or two and some addition to his royal revenues, kept his eyes on the interests of his young vassal who was also given assistance by Count Baldwin V of Flanders, a brother-in-law of the French King. In the autumn of 1046, when William was about eighteen, a full-scale rebellion began in western and middle Normandy headed by Guy of Burgundy who thought that he himself had a legitimate claim to the ducal throne. There is a story that an attempt was made to murder William, from which he escaped only by riding hell-for-leather to his birthplace of Falaise. He certainly sought for the protection and help of his overlord. At the beginning of 1047 King Henry I of France led an army into Normandy to the aid of his vassal. William raised some troops in eastern Normandy and joined Henry I; the western rebels were defeated in a confused battle at Val-ès-Dunes and in October of the same year Duke William

presided over an ecclesiastical council which agreed to impose the Truce of God on Normandy. Private wars were not permitted between Wednesday evening and Monday morning and were entirely prohibited during Advent, Lent, Easter and Pentecost. The King of France and the Duke of Normandy were exempted from the Truce of God, but anyone who violated it might incur the displeasure of the Church and be excommunicated. As a result of the battle and the truce the Norman rebels were temporarily abashed. According to William of Poitiers, the battle 'broke by iron the too arrogant heads, dismantled the ramparts of crime by victoriously

ABOVE Falaise in Normandy, where William was born, the bastard son of Duke Robert of Normandy by Herleve, a girl of that town. William probably spent his childhood at his mother's home in Falaise. The castle was built about a century after the birth of William.

recapturing many castles and thus stopped for a long time the intestinal wars in our region'. 'It was,' he added, 'a battle ... worthy of memory for many centuries to come.'

But in fact, the battle settled little. King Henry I, having done his bit for his vassal, departed from Normandy; Guy of Burgundy, though wounded, escaped from the field and fortified himself strongly in his castle at Brionne in central Normandy; and William, still only about twenty years old, had to contend with enemies outside as well as inside his duchy. He was obliged to subject Brionne to a close and elaborate siege; it was three years before Guy of Burgundy surrendered it upon terms and

The Viking Raids

During the ninth and tenth centuries much of northern Europe suffered from attacks from the Vikings, fierce Scandinavian warriors who were well ahead of the Christian nations in terms of military and naval skill. Many Danes and Norwegians settled in England and played an important part in English history in the tenth century. In 1027 King Canute proclaimed himself 'King of all England and Denmark and of Norway and part of Sweden', and although he soon lost his hold on Norway he maintained his control of England until his death. Not until well into the reign of William I did the Viking menace recede.

ABOVE The interior of a ninth-century Viking ship discovered at Gokstad in Norway.

LEFT The wooden prow of an eighth-century Viking ship discovered in Belgium. The prows of Viking ships were usually carved in the form of a snake's or a dragon's head.

RIGHT Viking ship and a whale, from a twelfth-century English Bestiary. The structure of Viking ships was adapted to short voyages, not violent seas: they were shallow, narrow in the beam, pointed at both ends and so very manœuvrable with oars. They had one large and heavy square sail and, on average, there were about forty men to a ship. (Bodleian Library, Ms Ashmole 1511, f. 86v.)

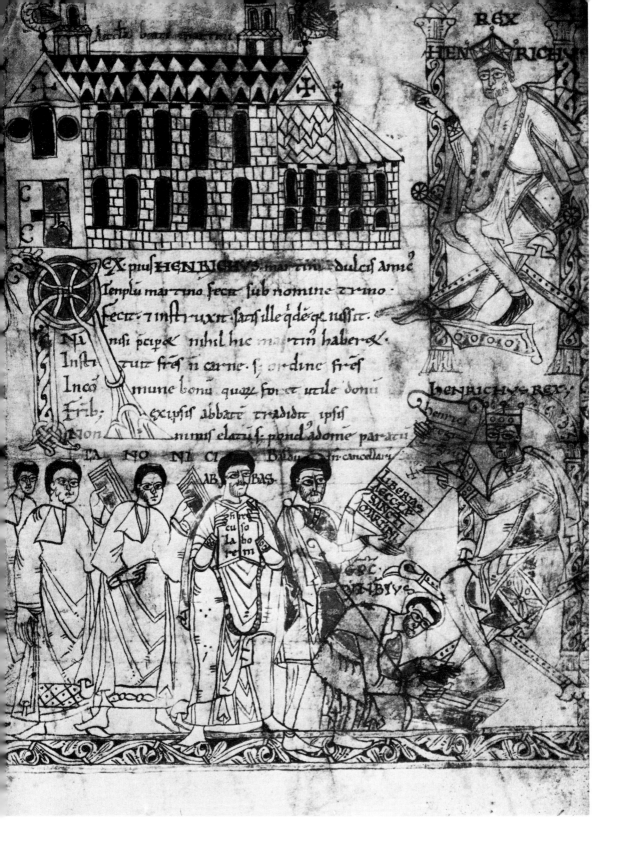

REX
HEN RICHS

X pius HENRICVS martino dulcis amic̄
Templu martino fecit sub nomine trino.
Fecit 7 instruxit satis ille q̄ dē ge iussit.
Nī nisi p̄cipē nihil hic martin haberet.
Instituit frēs n̄ carne. s̄ ordine frēs
Inco̅ mune bonū quæ foret utile donū
Frib; exipsis abbatē tradidit ipsis
Mon . mnis elati s̄ pond adom̄e parati

TA NO NI CI Baldw̄ cancellari
AB BAS
LIBERTAS ACCCLIE SINCTI MARTINI
GRC VNBIVS

HENRICVS REX
henrie

shre
cu so
la ho
rem

William was able to return to his capital of Rouen. Meanwhile, another soldier, as ambitious and ruthless as William himself proved to be, Geoffrey Martel, Count of Anjou, was occupied in expanding his territories. He advanced north and attacked the county of Maine, which lay to the south of Brittany and western Normandy. So masterful was he that when Count Hugh IV of Maine died, Geoffrey Martel was offered and accepted the succession. Once he had secured himself in Le Mans, the capital of Maine, he seized by force two castles, Domfront and Alençon, which stood just south of the Norman frontier and had long been in the hands of the lords of Bellême, who held them directly from the French King.

So partly for his own safety and partly to support the French King to whom he was under obligations, Duke William was practically compelled to make war upon the victorious Count of Anjou and Maine. He besieged Domfront, which he was unable to take by storm, but he managed to capture Alençon which was set on fire and those who mocked William as 'the tanner' had their limbs amputated. This so frightened the garrison at Domfront that they promptly surrendered under promise of mercy. William of Poitiers says that Duke William then declared, imitating the example of Julius Caesar: 'I came, I saw, I conquered.' Though he was able to strengthen the southern Norman frontier, he was aided in his victory by the fact that King Henry I of France had at the same time been threatening the position of Geoffrey Martel from the rear. But William's victories earned him a martial reputation far more impressive than he had gained from the secondary part he had played at the Battle of Val-ès-Dunes.

William's enhanced reputation enabled him to negotiate a marriage with Matilda, the daughter of Count Baldwin V of Flanders. Although Pope Leo IX for some reason or another forbade the proposed match, the wedding took place, probably in 1051. Not only did William thus provoke the Pope but he also managed to alienate his overlord, King Henry I. Possibly the French King thought that the young Duke was growing too big for his boots or was becoming ungrateful for his protection. At any rate Henry made a *volte-face* and allied himself with his former enemy, Geoffrey Martel. As William's two uncles – one of whom, Mauger, had succeeded Robert as

OPPOSITE Henry I, King of France until 1060. From 1047 until his death Henry was almost constantly at war with his vassal, Duke William of Normandy, who held his own against two royal invasions in 1054 and 1058.

59

Archbishop of Rouen and the other of whom, William, was Count of Talou – were both on bad terms with their nephew and ready to stir up trouble for him, William's position after his marriage was perilous in the extreme.

William was threatened by attack from both inside and outside Normandy. Moreover he was reluctant to make open war on his overlord, to whom he had strong reasons for gratitude, unless he was compelled to do so. His principal enemy in his own duchy was his uncle, William of Talou, the son of Duke Richard II by his second wife; the Count of Talou despised William the Bastard as an illegitimate heir to a throne which he thought should have been given to himself. He had deserted his nephew at the siege of Domfront, built himself a formidable castle at Arques on the borders of Normandy and France and evidently hoped to make himself supreme in eastern Normandy.

The castle of Arques was a masterpiece of military architecture and William was compelled to assemble a substantial army and subject it to a regular siege. He handed over the actual investment of the castle to one of his officers, while he himself took charge of a covering army which was ready to deal with any attempts at relief. William of Talou and Arques vainly appealed to King Henry I to come to his rescue. Henry certainly made an effort to do so, but whether because he was unwilling directly to fight his own vassal or whether he was dismayed by Duke William's effective isolation of the stronghold, he was unable to send either reinforcements or supplies to its aid. It took Duke William a long time to subdue this rebellion against his authority, but eventually at the end of 1053 he starved the garrison of Arques into surrender, promising only that the lives of the defenders would be spared, though his uncle was obliged to leave the duchy for ever.

It was not until the spring of 1054 that King Henry I of France openly attacked his Norman vassal. Had he done so earlier while the Count of Talou and Arques was still in arms, William might have succumbed to defeat. But after the fall of Arques he was able to gather together a large army with which to confront an invasion from the east by a considerable group of allies under the leadership of the French King. After devastating the countryside of eastern Normandy, a French force, demoralised by plunder and rape, reached the town of Mortemer, east of Neufchâtel in the modern *arrondissement* of the Lower Seine. Here the French were overwhelmed and cut to pieces by the Normans. Duke William himself took no part in the battle (for he had been engaged in warding off another threat to his capital of Rouen) but the victory was an organisational triumph for him. The King of France hastily quitted Normandy. William wisely returned such prisoners as had survived the battle. This victory, Professor Douglas has told us, has often been underestimated. It was, like the Battle of Hastings, a turning point in the career of William the Bastard. Moreover all the internal disturbances were at last at an end. For after his uncle William had been forced into exile, his other uncle, the Archbishop of Rouen, was deposed by a council over which William presided and which met at Lisieux in 1055.

The story of these years when William was under thirty were in a way a dress rehearsal for what was to happen in England over a decade later. The Battle of Mortemer was almost as decisive in William's career as that of Hastings; the overpowering of Count William of Talou and Arques by starving out the countryside was to be a precedent for King William's subduing of northern England.

Two years afterwards, Duke William frustrated another attempt by King Henry I, in alliance with Count Geoffrey Martel, to invade Normandy. By 1060 both these allies and enemies of William were dead and were succeeded by weaker men. In France, Philip I, who was still a child, became King and in Anjou, Geoffrey the Bearded, a nephew of Geoffrey Martel, succeeded. William was thus able to turn the tables and himself engaged in aggression against his neighbours. He arranged that his eldest son and heir, who was to be known as Robert 'Curthose' and was then about eleven, should be betrothed to Margaret, the sister of the young Count of Maine, Herbert II, who had by then replaced Geoffrey Martel. (In fact, Margaret died before the marriage could take place.) Herbert not only accepted William as his overlord but is said to have promised that if he died without issue, William should succeed him as Count. This story reads suspiciously like the story that Edward the Confessor had bequeathed his throne to William, and depends upon much the same authority. Just as in 1066

Duke William's troops attacking the castle of Dol in Brittany, while Conan II escapes by sliding down a rope; a scene from the Bayeux Tapestry.

William invaded England to lay claim to his alleged bequest from Edward the Confessor, so, after Herbert II's death in 1062, William invaded and devastated Maine and proclaimed himself Count. In 1064, William made a punitive raid into Brittany because the young Count there, Conan II, refused to acknowledge William as his overlord. It was on that expedition that William was accompanied, as has already been noted, by the future Harold II of England. Professor Barlow has written that 'It was hardly a glorious campaign. Harold ... may easily have

been contemptuous since he himself had just campaigned in similar circumstances and with more success, against Wales.' If so, Harold underestimated Duke William both as a soldier and as a politician.

The second half of the eleventh century was a tremendous period of Norman expansion in Europe. Robert Guiscard, one of the twelve sons of a minor Norman landowner, arrived with a handful of followers in Italy during 1047, and nine years later was joined by his younger brother Roger. Together they

overran much of southern Italy and Sicily, and a defeat was inflicted on Pope Leo IX (the Pope who had banned Duke William's marriage) at Civitate, thirty miles north of Foggia. Roger, after the death of his brother, not only completed the conquest of Sicily but captured the island of Malta; and an illegitimate son of Robert Guiscard, Bohemund by name, proved himself an outstanding general, took part in the First Crusade, captured Antioch in Asia Minor, of which he became the prince, and menaced the eastern empire at Constantinople.

The eleventh century was a tremendous period of Norman expansion and Robert Guiscard, the son of a Norman landowner, conquered Apulia, Calabria and Sicily. An illegitamate son of his took part in the First Crusade which started in 1096 and succeeded in capturing Antioch. RIGHT A Crusader army on the move. OPPOSITE A warrior in Jeruslam c. 1109.

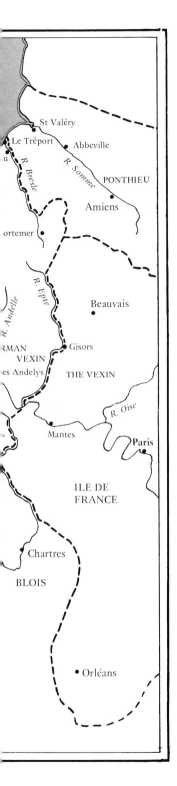

But Duke William's successes in conquering Maine and England and in repelling the enemies on his frontiers in Anjou and Brittany, Scotland and Wales were the finest examples of the expansion of Norman power.

What was the character of Normandy from the administrative and cultural point of view when William, twenty-five years after he had been acknowledged as Duke, had beaten off all his enemies and given his government a firm and virtually unchallenged position? It used to be argued that a definite 'feudal system' had been created in Normandy in which the magnates of the realm were granted lands in return for undertaking to provide the services of armed knights whenever the Duke required them. But that was hardly the case. 'Feudalism', a word not invented until the seventeenth century, was, if it existed at all, in a state of flux in Normandy. The question will be examined in more detail later (see Chapter 5). William as Duke was served by counts and viscounts. The first Norman rulers were, it seems, called counts, but when their status was raised to that of duke, counts, usually members of the ducal family, became in effect responsible for the administration of specific areas of the duchy and were stationed in border areas in which they could not only ensure local security but be ready to defend their country if it were attacked from the outside. The viscounts were not, as might be supposed, the deputies of the counts. They were, on the contrary, accountable to the Duke in administrative districts throughout the whole of Normandy for the execution of justice and the collection of taxes. Viscounts, like counts, also had duties to perform in time of war. Although both counts and viscounts lived in castles, few Norman castles were not under direct ducal authority. The private castles that were later to be found in England scarcely existed in Normandy. William saw to it that 'illicit castles' were suppressed. Though naturally he took into consideration the advice of his nobility, William was the effective ruler of Normandy. A full council of the ducal court might meet from time to time, but not with the regularity of the English Witanegemot. The Norman council would be attended by the leading lay and ecclesiastical lords and by the Duchess and her sons. The Duke's staff included stewards (the most important officials), chamberlains, butlers and a chancellor, but there was no organised chancery as in

England. Nor did the ducal court have a monopoly of justice since in a few instances jurisdiction had passed into private hands.

The maintenance of the Duke's authority therefore depended largely upon his own character, strength and wisdom. Vassalage was not of great significance at that time. For example, although William himself was the vassal of the French King, he was entirely independent in his own duchy. Nor had the Duke been able to impose upon his own vassals specific and recognisable obligations to him. Lower down the scale there were *fideles* or liegemen. But the elaborate dues and reliefs that were defined later in feudal England (for example in Magna Carta) are scarcely referred to in contemporary Norman charters. William relied upon a group of secular and ecclesiastical lords on whom he conferred gifts (such as lands confiscated from his enemies) to serve him loyally and with whom he had friendly personal relations. But, as Professor David Douglas, one of the greatest authorities on and admirers of early Normandy, has stated, 'there seems little warranty for believing that anything resembling tenure by knight-service, in the later sense of the term, was uniformly established, or carefully defined, in pre-Conquest Normandy'. Nevertheless the idea was growing. If no specific *servitium debitum* – service owed to the Duke by his secular nobility – is to be seen, towards the middle of his reign, contractual military service was required from some Norman monasteries and some Norman bishoprics. Also, William was in the process of creating a new lay aristocracy, personally loyal to him. When, on his conquest of England, he had at his disposal a huge fund of confiscated lands, it was natural for him to reward his followers – 'the companions of the Conqueror' – but to expect from them in return specified military services.

'The companions of the Conqueror'

In Normandy, neither the secular nor the ecclesiastical nobility (they were rarely called barons) exerted enormous influence. The archbishops of Rouen, as has been observed, were administrators who performed many services for the Duke. But most of the bishops were neither particularly pious nor chaste. The religious life of the country was chiefly influenced by the monks. The revived form of Benedictine monasticism, which spread from the model monastery of Cluny in Burgundy, reached Normandy via Fécamp and became dominant. Some earlier monasteries, not under Cluniac influence, already existed in Normandy, notably those of Mont St Michel and Jumièges, but during the reign of Duke William over twenty new monasteries were founded in which both William and his wife took an active interest. Two new houses (for monks and nuns) were established on ducal demesne land at Caen. The men's monastery, St Stephen's, was endowed by the Duke and the nunnery, Holy Trinity, by the Duchess. These however were established as a penance imposed upon them by Pope Nicholas II for their uncanonical marriage. Lanfranc of Pavia, a man of impressive learning, was appointed abbot of the monastery as a reward because it was he who persuaded the Pope to change his mind and grant a dispensation for William's marriage, which had incurred the disapproval of Rome for so long. Not only did the Duke thus sponsor and care for Norman monasteries but he attended all ecclesiastical councils such as the one at which his uncle Mauger, Archbishop of Rouen, was condemned, and sanctioned their decrees.

The dukes of Normandy had always enjoyed the right of nominating bishops and abbots. After the deposition of Mauger, William appointed Maurilius, who was not a Norman but had been born in Rheims and was a saintly man, to be Archbishop of Rouen. Maurilius was a keen practitioner of monastic reform. As head of the abbey of Bec, which Lanfranc had earlier transformed into a centre of serious study, William appointed Anselm of Aosta, another saintly character, who was to become Archbishop of Canterbury during the reign of William Rufus. But Maurilius, Lanfranc and Anselm were scarcely typical of the bishops and abbots appointed by Duke William. Most of them were his friends and relations. For example, he made his half-brother Odo, Bishop of Bayeux: Odo was more of a soldier than a churchman and his appointment has been described as a piece of flagrant nepotism. Moreover, bishops and abbots were expected to pay for their favours. Some of the secular aristocracy who founded monasteries regarded them as a valuable form of investment: they allotted estates in return for annual payments by the monasteries, thus arranging a compromise between God and Mammon. Still, the intellectual life of Normandy undoubtedly owed almost everything to the monasteries, where history (however unreliable) was written, medicine studied and practised, music and poetry cultivated and

The island abbey of Mont St Michel, founded in 966 by Duke Richard I of Normandy.

OPPOSITE The ruins of the abbey church of Jumièges, a powerful religious centre in the eleventh century.

architecture revolutionised. New cathedrals and monastic churches were built with Romanesque towers and Byzantine mosaics, apsidal choirs and chapels.

William of Poitiers, who was the Duke's deepest admirer, wrote that even though he had to suppress wars at home and abroad as well as preventing brigandage and pillage, he never forgot his duty to God or his country. He never 'undertook an unjust war' and by his repressive laws he was able to deliver Normandy from thieves, murderers and other criminals. This

70

was in fact fair comment upon William's strict government, for, as in England, he showed himself capable of imposing internal peace and security. 'The countryside, the castles and the towns found in him a guarantor of stability and safety for their possessions,' William of Poitiers added. The Duke enforced the Truce of God, he checked all outbursts of violence and he protected the poor, the widows and the orphans. It is an impressive, if somewhat exaggerated tribute.

In considering the character of Normandy during the first twenty years in which William reigned over it, one has to appreciate that the duchy was smaller, poorer and less fertile than England: it was roughly equal in size to the earldom of Wessex and its population must have been comparably lower. Moreover, in spite of the vicissitudes which England had experienced from the time of the original Anglo-Saxon in-

In expiation of their uncanonical marriage, William I and Queen Matilda founded two great abbeys in Caen. ABOVE LEFT The Abbaye-aux-Hommes founded by William. ABOVE RIGHT The crypt of the Abbaye-aux-Dames founded by Matilda.

vasions to that of Edward the Confessor, its culture and civilisation had been maintained at a high level. King Alfred the Great, who ruled in England in the ninth century, was an infinitely more cultured and versatile character than Rolf the Viking, founder of Normandy. If Rolf was converted to Christianity at the beginning of the tenth century, England had been largely Christianised since the seventh century. Alfred not only united the English kingdom and codified its laws but promoted religion, learning and education; unlike William, he was no great believer in monasticism. He thought it 'important to translate the books which are most needful for all men into the language which we can all understand'. Alfred, like William, was a considerable general (he also built a navy) and it was his defeat of the Danish onslaught that helped to preserve Christian civilisation in early Europe. The late Sir Frank

King Alfred the Great portrayed on the ninth-century Alfred Jewel, made of gold and decorated with *cloisonné* enamel. He was the greatest of the Anglo-Saxon Kings: he united England, codified its laws and encouraged religion and learning.

Stenton once wrote that 'in comparison with England, Normandy in the mid-eleventh century was a state in the making'.

It is therefore difficult to argue that the duchy of Normandy was more advanced politically or culturally than the England of Edward the Confessor and Earl Harold of Wessex (this point will be developed later). Professor Douglas wrote:

> During the decades preceding the Norman conquest of England, the aristocratic and ecclesiastical development of Normandy had been merged under the rule of Duke William II into a single political achievement. It might perhaps be summarised by saying that in 1065 a man could go from end to end of the duchy without ever

74

passing outside the jurisdiction, secular or ecclesiastical, of a small group of interrelated great families with the Duke at their head.

To that extent it is true that William had unified his kingdom by promoting his relations and friends to key posts. As the late Sir Winston Churchill remarked, there is a great deal to be said for favouritism.

But what undoubtedly emerged was that Duke William had become an energetic, experienced and effective ruler and leader. Like Robert and Roger Guiscard, he found himself vigorous enough and forcible enough to invade and subdue a country bigger and more cultured than his own. There was nothing in either the economic resources or the military experience of the duchy to make his victory certain. It was the quality of the Duke himself – his own energy and control of his men and resources – that explains the Norman conquest of England.

3
How England was Subdued
1067-87

WHEN WILLIAM RETURNED to Normandy in March 1067 he took all the obvious precautions over the security of England. He left behind him two joint regents: his half-brother, Odo, Bishop of Bayeux, who had become Earl of Kent, an ambitious, dangerous and licentious character, and William fitz Osbern, formerly one of the Duke's stewards in Normandy, who was related to and fully trusted by his master and became Earl of Hereford. Both these regents were provided with armies: Odo was intended to look after southern England, and fitz Osbern was given responsibility for the unruly north. According to Ordericus Vitalis, a monkish chronicler who lived in Normandy and wrote during the next century, both the regents acted in an extremely provocative manner and so did their underlings: 'the petty lords' who were guarding the newly built castles 'oppressed all the inhabitants of high and lower degree,' he wrote, 'and heaped shameful burdens upon them'. Soldiers were allowed to loot and rape. The contemporary Anglo-Saxon Chronicler says briefly: 'Bishop Odo and Earl William were left behind here, and they built castles far and wide throughout the land, oppressing the unhappy people, and things went ever from bad to worse.' According to Ordericus again, the regents were so swollen with pride that they refused to listen to reasonable complaints from the English or to give them impartial justice.

As a precaution, William took back with him to Normandy as hostages Prince Edgar, Morcar and Edwin, who were still Earls of Northumbria and Mercia but had been virtually suspended from their offices, Stigand, Archbishop of Canterbury, Waltheof, a son of a former Earl of Northumbria, who was Earl of Huntingdon and neighbouring counties, and (according to the *Anglo-Saxon Chronicle*) 'many other good men from England'. Thus, William evidently hoped that he had removed all the English leaders who might have formed the nuclei of revolts against the Norman government.

However, the ruthlessness and obnoxiousness of the regents inevitably brought about isolated outbreaks. The first revolt was directed by a curious character named Edric the Wild about whom little is known: he is said to have come one night upon the fairies dancing and to have fallen in love with one of them, whom he married. The attack originated in Wales and aimed

PREVIOUS PAGES Dover Castle, one of the first castles built on William's orders in England after the Battle of Hastings.

78

to capture the newly-built Norman castle at Hereford. But Edric and his Welsh companions failed to take the castle and soon retired with their booty back into Wales. A more serious rising took place in Kent. The Kentishmen invited over Count Eustace of Boulogne, who had fought on William's side at the Battle of Hastings and was familiar with Dover from the famous incident of 1051. Odo had been given particular charge of the port by William, but he was absent in the north at the time of Eustace's arrival. Eustace and his men occupied the town of Dover, but were unable to overcome the garrison of the castle, which was one of the first castles to be built on William's orders in England. Eustace therefore withdrew thwarted. But it was then rumoured that the Northumbrians had invoked the aid of King Swein, known as Estrithson, who was the nephew of the former King Canute of England and had with some difficulty established himself as King of Denmark after the death of Canute's son, Harthacnut. It was possibly on account of these rumours that William I returned to England from Normandy on St Nicholas's day, 6 December 1067.

The first thing that William did, however, after his return, was to suppress a rising in south-west England. He led an army containing English as well as Norman soldiers into Devon and Cornwall. He laid siege to Exeter, the capital of Devon. Although the local thegns deserted them, the townspeople put up fierce resistance which lasted eighteen days; the Duke's army suffered severe losses. Consequently, William allowed the city to surrender on terms, which he appears to have honoured, although the Anglo-Saxon Chronicler remarks sourly that 'he made favourable promises to the citizens which were badly kept'. Harold's mother and illegitimate sons were in Exeter but managed to escape before the capitulation. William ordered a castle to be built and left behind a garrison to guard against further unrest. In due course, the towns of Bristol and Gloucester also yielded. William kept Easter at Winchester, and Whitsun at Westminster. He thought that England was now sufficiently pacified to invite his Duchess to join him. She was crowned Queen in Westminster Abbey.

In fact, while the south of England from Exeter to Dover was completely under Norman control, neither the Midlands nor the north were yet prepared to settle down under the new

'Favourable promises … which were badly kept'

regime. William had brought back his hostages, and as he must have foreseen, they quickly became leaders of revolts. Prince Edgar, for example, fled to the Court of King Malcolm III in Scotland. Malcolm was the successor of Macbeth, of Shakespearian fame, who had in fact governed Scotland admirably for seventeen years. Malcolm married as his second wife Margaret, Edgar's sister, by whom he had six sons. Margaret was not anxious to marry, but Malcolm was an ardent suitor. Margaret 'swore she would be no man's bride. Nor his, should the Celestial Mercy ordain her heart within her flesh to keep in maidenhood and purest continence in this brief life her Mighty Lord to please.' However, as the Anglo-Saxon Chronicler continued, 'it came to pass as directed by God's Providence: it could not be otherwise, just as He Himself says in his Gospel, that not even one sparrow can fall into a snare without His forethought'.

So it was hardly surprising that Edgar should hope for help at his future brother-in-law's Court. About the same time, the Northumbrians, who were rarely passive, found leaders to head a rebellion against the Normans. Not only was their former earl, Morcar, hostile to the King, but Gospatric, their new earl, though he had bought his earldom from William, was of English noble blood and a former friend of Tostig, brother of Harold II. The Northumbrians sought aid both from Malcolm III and from King Swein of Denmark. So in the summer or autumn of 1068 William thought it advisable himself to direct a campaign to subdue the Midlands and the north-east.

As with his capture of London in 1066, William did not march directly upon York. First he went to Warwick and thence to Nottingham. He was able to enter York without meeting any resistance; he appears to have been assisted by the Archbishop of York, Aldred. As Aldred is reputed to have crowned Harold II and at one time to have advocated Edgar becoming King, he was clearly a clergyman extremely versatile in his allegiances. The local magnates hastened to submit, and Malcolm III sent a message promising his fealty, at any rate for the time being. William returned to London by way of Lincoln, Huntingdon and Cambridge, all of which yielded to him. Everywhere he ordered castles to be built. When he reached southern England, William dispatched a Norman, Robert of

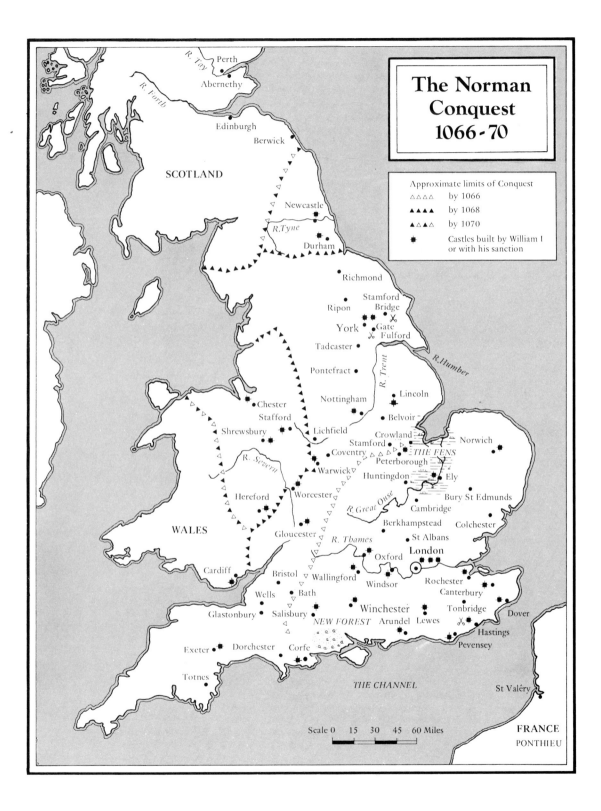

The Norman Conquest 1066-70

Approximate limits of Conquest
△ △ △ △ by 1066
▲ ▲ ▲ ▲ by 1068
▲ △ ▲ △ by 1070
✠ Castles built by William I or with his sanction

SCOTLAND

R. Tay
Perth
Abernethy
R. Forth
Edinburgh
Berwick
Newcastle
R. Tyne
Durham
Richmond
Stamford Bridge
Ripon
York
Gate Fulford
Tadcaster
Pontefract
R. Trent
R. Humber
Chester
Stafford
Shrewsbury
Lichfield
Nottingham
Lincoln
Belvoir
Crowland
Stamford
Norwich
Coventry
THE FENS
Peterborough
Warwick
Ely
Huntingdon
Hereford
Worcester
Bury St Edmunds
R. Great Ouse
Cambridge
WALES
Gloucester
Berkhampstead
Colchester
R. Thames
St Albans
Oxford
London
Cardiff
Bristol
Wallingford
Rochester
Canterbury
Wells
Bath
Windsor
Glastonbury
Salisbury
Winchester
Tonbridge
Dover
NEW FOREST
Arundel
Lewes
Exeter
Dorchester
Corfe
Hastings
Pevensey
Totnes
THE CHANNEL
St Valéry
Scale 0   15   30   45   60 Miles
FRANCE
PONTHIEU

Norman Castles

There were few castles in pre-Conquest England but after 1066 a big castle-building programme was started by the Normans. Domesday Book mentions some fifty castles in England and Wales, but there were at least eighty-four castles in England by the end of the eleventh century. The network of castles provided focal points for military power and local government, and helped to maintain and extend the Conquest. Originally a device of war, the castles became a permanent feature of the new feudal administrative order which the Normans established.

ABOVE LEFT The entrance to Colchester castle begun on William's orders during his reign.

ABOVE RIGHT Chepstow castle in Monmouthshire. William fitz Osbern planted a colony at Chepstow as part of the Norman penetration of Wales.

LEFT Pevensey Castle, the first castle built by William in England. It was started after he landed at Pevensey with his invasion force.

RIGHT The White Tower, the central keep of the Tower of London, the most impressive military monument of the Norman Conquest.

Commines, to replace Gospatric as Earl of Northumbria; he trusted Earl Robert to keep the whole of the north in order.

The year 1069 was the most perilous during William's entire reign in England. In January, the new Earl of Northumbria, whom the King had personally selected to take full charge of the north, was burned to death in the bishop's palace at Durham, along with nine hundred of his men, according to the *Anglo-Saxon Chronicle*. A spontaneous rising again took place in York, where the Norman commander of the castle was put to death. Edgar came down from Scotland, with the approval of his brother-in-law, and received an enthusiastic welcome from the local inhabitants. Moreover two of Harold's sons carried out piratic raids on the south-west coast of England. But King William moved with exceptional speed. He came up from the south unexpectedly with an overwhelming host, routed the rebels in York, and slew several hundreds of those who could not escape. This time he handed the city over to the plunder of his soldiers. Edgar discreetly retired to Scotland.

Although William had shattered the rebels and had acted so quickly that he had surprised them before they were ready for his coming, and therefore was able to return south in time for Easter, the rebellion kindled the hopes of the English elsewhere. The men of Dorset and Somerset rose in arms, and two of Harold II's remaining sons reached north Devon from Ireland. There were also uprisings based on North Wales and Chester, whence Shropshire was attacked, while other disturbances took place in the Midlands. King William's local commanders proved capable of coping with the emergency. The invaders from Ireland were driven out; Exeter remained intact; Shrewsbury, though burned to the ground, was abandoned by the King's enemies. But in the autumn, the King's authority was more dangerously menaced, this time from abroad. King Swein of Denmark, who had been in contact with the discontented in the north of England, sent over a fleet under two of his sons and one of his brothers. This expedition was not in fact as big as that sent by Harold Hardrada of Norway against King Harold II in 1066. Probing attacks were made on the southern and eastern coasts, and eventually the Danish ships entered the Humber. A general rising took place in Yorkshire which was joined by most of William's principal enemies including Prince Edgar, Earl Gospatric and on this occasion Earl Waltheof, one of the few English magnates who had won William's confidence. York fell to the Danes on 20 September 1069 and some of them penetrated into Lincolnshire.

Once more, William was faced with a major crisis and again he personally took control. The King first moved north and drove the Danes out of Lincolnshire and back into Yorkshire. Then he turned west and dealt effectively with a rising on the Welsh borders, again led by Edric the Wild. The King next moved into the Midlands and from his base in Nottingham began a systematic devastation of the north with the main objects of depriving the Danes of supplies and disconcerting their English allies. He was held up for three weeks when trying to cross the River Aire at Pontefract before a ford was discovered, but finally he reached and took York. William decided not to return to the south, but celebrated Christmas in York, determined afterwards to carry through a winter campaign.

First, he forced his way across the Pennines and occupied Chester, the principal centre of resistance to his rule in north-west England, and also took Stafford. Both the Mercians and the Northumbrians lost heart. Edgar again withdrew to Scotland, and Earl Waltheof made his peace with the King. The Danes were discouraged and accepted a bribe to leave the country. In 1070, according to the Anglo-Saxon Chronicler, 'the King had all the monasteries in England plundered and in this same year there was a great famine'. A later chronicler spoke of both good and bad being ruined by 'a consuming famine' and used the words 'a wholesale massacre'. Professor Douglas tells us that the campaign of 1069–70 'must rank as one of the outstanding military achievements of the age'. When William finally reached Winchester at Easter, he disbanded part of his army in the belief that England was at last subjugated. Some of his mercenaries were paid off, and the women of Normandy demanded that their husbands should return home.

'There was a great famine'

Nonetheless, all was not yet quite over, for the Danish fleet had been allowed to remain at anchor off the Humber during the winter and it was reinforced there in the spring of 1070 by the arrival of King Swein himself with additional ships. This time, no attempt was made to conquer devastated Northumbria, but the Danes turned their attention to Lincolnshire; Peter-

85

borough was sacked and the Isle of Ely was occupied as a base. There the Danes were joined by Earl Morcar and a number of Englishmen who were discontented, including a mysterious hero known as Hereward the Wake, a local Lincolnshire thegn. But in June, King William and King Swein concluded a treaty of peace. Swein promised to withdraw his ships from the Humber and his soldiers from Lincolnshire, taking with them all the loot that they had collected from Ely and elsewhere, comprising, among other things, 'a diadem all of pure gold from Our Lord's head'. Hereward held out in the fen country for more than a year; but Earl Morcar was taken prisoner and died, while his brother Edwin was killed by his own followers when attempting to flee to Scotland. Thus these two singularly unimpressive English earls met their end. When William himself eventually came to Ely, the rebels were compelled to surrender, but Hereward escaped and disappears from recorded history.

One further action had to be taken by William to ensure the quiet and safety of his kingdom, and that was to check incursions from Wales and Scotland. Along the borders of Wales, William instituted earls, who in return for compact territories granted to them undertook to guard the threatened frontiers. The King

86

had appointed his steward, William fitz Osbern, Earl of Hereford, and later two other Normans were made Earls of Chester and Shrewsbury. William fitz Osbern managed to get himself killed in Flanders in 1071 and was succeeded as Earl of Hereford by his second son, Roger of Breteuil, who later became mixed up in a conspiracy against the King and was thrown into prison in 1075. So in 1081, William was obliged himself to penetrate into Wales, where he built a castle at Cardiff. On the whole, the frontier earldoms worked well enough, although the Welsh were to be a running sore in the side of English kings at least until the reign of Edward I.

Scotland presented different problems. The boundary between England and Scotland had never been clearly defined; the Scots kings at their most expansive claimed that Cumbria included Cumberland and Westmorland, and Lothian comprised much of Northumbria. William was compelled to intervene in Scotland partly because Malcolm III had in 1070 been harrying the north of England when William's attentions had been distracted elsewhere; also, as has been noted, Malcolm married a sister of Prince Edgar, who still regarded himself as the legitimate heir to the English throne. Malcolm was an able ruler, who, after defeating Macbeth, governed his country fairly successfully for thirty-five years, although some of his subjects were of the opinion that he was too much under English influence through his second wife. But Malcolm did not possess the resources to resist the full flood of William's wrath. In August, the King of England planned an elaborate campaign against his northern neighbour. He led an army through Lothian and crossed the Forth by a ford, and then advanced onwards through Fife towards Perth, north of the River Tay. Simultaneously a fleet was despatched along the east coast of England to enter the Tay and *rendezvous* with the land forces. Evidently William aspired to overwhelm the Scots. But Malcolm thought discretion was the better part of valour. As the Anglo-Saxon Chronicler succinctly put it, 'King Malcolm came and made his peace with King William [at Abernethy], gave hostages and became his vassal, and the King returned home with his levies.' The precise terms of the Treaty of Abernethy (on the south side of the Tay) are not known. It is certain, however, that Malcolm gave his eldest son as hostage

A view of the River Tay, on the
south side of which, at Abernethy,
William and Malcolm made
a treaty, Malcolm recognising
William as his overlord and
giving William his eldest son
as a hostage for the Scots King's
good behaviour.

Robert Curthose,
William's eldest son; a
detail from his tomb in
Gloucester Cathedral.

and expelled his brother-in-law from his Court. The frontiers
do not appear to have been defined and Malcolm awaited a
more favourable opportunity to badger the English kings.

William must have been glad to have got this question
settled, for problems were awaiting him in France. Before his
expedition against the Scots, William had paid a flying visit to
Normandy to examine the situation. The chief threat came
from Maine. The position there was somewhat anomalous, for
the Conqueror had conferred the title of Count of Maine on his

son Robert Curthose. Now a rival emerged named Fulk le Rechin, who was already Count of Anjou. As Robert was still a minor, Fulk had no difficulty in attracting support, including that of Geoffrey, Lord of Mayenne. In 1069 and again in 1070 the citizens of Le Mans revolted against the Normans. Problems also arose for William east of Normandy. In the summer of 1070, Count Baldwin VI of Flanders, William's brother-in-law, died and his widow took over as Regent. William then sent his steward, William fitz Osbern, to look after his interests in Flanders, but he was defeated and killed by the Regent's rival, Robert le Frison (so called because he came from Frisia in Holland). Thus Flanders had become hostile and Maine was in revolt. As soon as he had settled his affairs in the north of England, William led a large army, in which Englishmen as well as Normans served, south from Normandy into Maine. The campaign began so early in 1073 that the rebels were taken almost completely by surprise and Le Mans was captured without difficulty. Robert Curthose had by then come of age and was left in control of the county.

William's victory in Maine really marked the apogee of his military career. Afterwards, his enemies on both sides of the Channel constantly plotted and fought against him. Even his eldest son, Robert, turned against his father, demanding that he should be allowed to take up what he regarded as his rightful and promised position as full Duke of Normandy. Consequently, William had little time to spend in England, where he relied particularly on Lanfranc, who replaced Stigand as Archbishop of Canterbury in 1070, Stigand having been deposed with the agreement of Pope Alexander II.

But the many enemies that William conjured up caused his situation to become increasingly hazardous. The King of France was determined to hold in check the ruler of what historians sometimes call, not altogether happily, 'the Anglo-Norman kingdom'. An obvious rival to William in England was Prince Edgar, who was used as a pawn by all William's foes. After an agreeable but fruitless visit to Scotland (Malcolm III kept the terms of the Treaty of Abernethy by refusing him help), Edgar was patronised by King Philip I of France who offered him a castle from which he might engineer mischief. But King William recognised the feebleness of his rival. He arranged for him to be collected from the north of England by the sheriff of York, treated with every consideration and brought over to the Court of Normandy. There, in the words of the Anglo-Saxon Chronicler, 'King William received him with great ceremony, and then he remained at the King's Court … and accepted such privileges as he granted him.'

A far more dangerous enemy of the King was a Breton magnate known as Ralph de Gael who was also Earl of Norfolk. Some time in 1075, King William had permitted the Earl, who by birth was half-Breton and half-English, to marry a sister of Roger, Earl of Hereford, son of King William's once trusted but now dead steward, William fitz Osbern. Among those invited to the wedding were Waltheof, Earl of Huntingdon, an Englishman, and a number of Bretons. These three earls took it into their heads to plan a conspiracy against the King under the cover of the wedding celebrations. William was to be distracted by disturbances on the Breton-Norman frontier; a rebellion against the King's regents was plotted in the English Midlands; and the future King Canute IV of Denmark was to be invited to land a large piratical force on the east coast. What precisely the conspirators expected to gain from all this is obscure and in any case the rebellion failed. William remained in western Normandy to prevent trouble there. Roger was unable to advance eastwards from Herefordshire and Ralph was equally obstructed in Norfolk: so, leaving the defence of Norwich castle to his wife, Earl Ralph left the country. In due course, Norwich surrendered to William's regents and by the time the Danes arrived, the rebellion in England was already crushed. Thus, before William himself landed in England at Christmas 1075, the revolt of the three earls had long been at an end. Earl Roger was put into prison and kept there until he died. Earl Waltheof was beheaded outside Winchester in May 1076; the Anglo-Saxon Chronicler wrote a little poem about the fate of the Bretons concerned:

> Some of them were blinded,
> Some of them were banished,
> So all traitors to William
> Were laid low.

Only Earl Ralph was left alive in Brittany to carry on the struggle against his overlord.

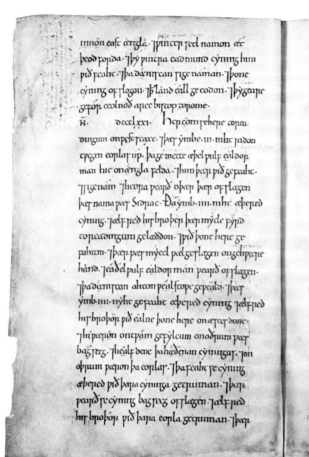

Earl Ralph entered into an alliance with Geoffrey Grannon, who claimed to be the Count of Brittany, and they fortified themselves in the castle of Dol near the Norman frontier. King William, acting in association with Hoel, Count of Cornouailles, who, as the son-in-law of the previous Count, asserted that he was now the rightful heir, laid siege to Dol. King Philip of France perceived his opportunity and, advancing from Poitou, relieved Dol, compelling William to retreat into Normandy, losing many of his men and much of his treasure. This defeat, wrote Professor Douglas, 'was the first military check that he [William] suffered in France for more than twenty years and its importance has been unduly minimized'.

For the time being, compromises were arranged and complicated feudal relationships patched up. But William then

A page from the *Anglo-Saxon Chronicle*, an invaluable source of early English history which deals with events from the invasion of Julius Caesar in 55 BC to the accession of Henry II in 1154.

93

OPPOSITE William
enthroned, an illustration
from an eleventh-century
manuscript.

met with difficulties from his son, a squabble between two generations not infrequent in the history of English kings. These quarrels are vividly pictured by the monk Ordericus Vitalis in his *Ecclesiastical History*. He describes Robert, who was twenty-five, as 'talkative and prodigal, very bold and valiant' with a loud voice and a fluent tongue; because his body was stout and stature short he had been nicknamed 'Curthose' (short boots) or 'Gamberon' (round-legged). He demanded from his father full authority in Normandy and Maine (where the Count of Anjou was his overlord). William, now in his fifties, had ruled Normandy for thirty years as well as England for ten. He refused even to meet his son half-way, and said that what he wanted was 'preposterous'. 'It was by Norman valour that I made the conquest of England,' he told Robert, 'Normandy is mine by hereditary descent and I will never while I live relinquish the government.' His eldest son, thus disappointed, after vainly trying to surprise Rouen, threw in his lot with the French King and discontented elements in Brittany, Maine and Anjou. At Christmas 1078, these uncongenial allies inflicted a defeat on William and it is related that Robert wounded his father in a battle fought at Gerberoy near the eastern frontier of Normandy. Thenceforward, difficulties mounted for the ageing King. A great battle between the Angevins and Bretons on one side and the Normans and English troops on the other was prevented only by the Church:

> While [wrote Ordericus Vitalis] the two armies were in face of each other, drawn out for battle, and many hearts quailed at the fearful death, and still more fearful fate after death which awaits the reprobate, a cardinal priest of the Roman Church and some pious monks, intervened by divine inspiration, and remonstrated with the chiefs of both armies.

That was in 1080. As before, in 1077, some sort of compromise was arranged. Robert was by now reconciled to his father, but in 1082 William quarrelled with his half-brother Odo, Bishop of Bayeux, who had apparently been planning an expedition of his own to Italy with the grandiose aim of becoming Pope in succession to the famous Gregory VII (who in fact lived until 1085). William put Odo under arrest 'in order to curb his restless ambition', and he was imprisoned in the castle of Rouen until his brother died. But the last military services performed

Incipit lib̄ de S̄c̄au̅ ċc̄ℓie Belℓ.
& de Possessionib̅ s̄ibi d Rege Witt̅o
& ab alii̅ q̄ libet
datic̄s :~

NO̅ AB̅ N̅
CARꞂATIОꞂE D̅ꞂI. ꞃ̅

Lxvi. Dux Ꞃormannoru̅
nobilissimus Willelmus
cu̅ manu ualida pugna
toru̅ in Angliam trans
nauigauit. uꞇ regnu̅

q̅q̅ sibi a suo consanguineo
Rege Eadwardo dimissum. de ma
nu ꞃaraldi q̅ illud tiraннica frau
de inuaserat abstraeret: sibiq̅ illud
iure hereditario possidendu̅ obtineret.
ꞃoc audito ꞃaraldus cu̅ exercitu con
c illu̅ aduenit. duce strenuissimo Witt̅o
audacter inde ei cu̅ exercitu ad locu̅ q̅ n̅c
Bellu̅ uocatur occurrente. Dux g̅ deuotus
in p̅cinctu bellico ia̅ Armatus. conuocatis
Baronibus & militibus suis uniuersos. exor
tatione sua & spe p̅missionu̅ fiducialiter
monet pugnę insistere: atq; ad eorum
corda roboranda cora̅ eis cu̅ fauore omniu̅
uotu̅ deo fecit. uꞇ si diuina pietas illi

in England by William were on its frontiers. The King himself had found time to lead his expedition against the Welsh, and Robert, acting for his father, compelled Malcolm III, King of the Scots, to renew the pact of Abernethy.

How was it that William had been able to subject the English to his will? He did not manage it merely by winning the Battle of Hastings. It took him from five to six years to complete his conquest. Was he then a magnificent organiser and a military genius? On the whole, he was successful in selecting reliable lieutenants, mainly Normans or other Frenchmen who, although they may have lined their pockets, did their master's will. It is questionable if William was a first-class commander: the setbacks in the later part of his reign reveal that. But first it needs to be noted that when he was younger he acted with such swiftness and boldness to quell centres of resistance that he was often upon his enemies before they expected him. His handling of mounted troops was particularly effective. Secondly, good use was made of castles as fortified strongpoints to hold down the surrounding country. These castles were less common in Normandy than once used to be supposed, but they were largely introduced into England by William. They could be built quickly, as they consisted at first simply of an earthen 'motte' or mound, surrounded by a ditch and crowned with a wooden tower; a bailey or defensive area, also usually fortified by earthen ramparts, lay beneath. These motte-and-bailey castles were commanded by castellans whom the King trusted. They were distributed throughout the kingdom in strategically significant areas. It has been estimated that by the end of William's reign, over eighty castles had been built and some of them were already being reconstructed in stone.

In the third place, William ruled by terror. In his campaign of 1070 he consciously set out to devastate the old earldoms of Mercia and Northumbria to such an extent that they could never again become centres of resistance to his supremacy. Churches were burned down, monasteries were plundered and agricultural land was systematically laid waste. As Sir Frank Stenton wrote, 'The operations of 1069–70 were distinguished from ordinary warfare by a deliberate attempt to ruin the population of the affected districts ... within the country ravaged at this time vast areas were still derelict after seventeen

OPPOSITE William's son-in-law, Alan of Brittany, swearing allegiance to William for the lands of Edwin, the former Saxon Earl of Mercia. By ousting the Saxon lords and giving their lands to his Norman friends and relations, William strengthened his hold over the English.

Ego Willms cognoie Bastard? Rex Anglie do 7
cedo tibi Nepoti meo Alano Britanie comiti
7 hrediby tuis impetm omes villas 7 tras que
nup fuerut Comitis Edwyni in Eboracshi
7 inscutudis; ita libe 7 honorifice sicut ide
Edwi ea tenuit. Dat in ossesione coram
Civitate Ebor

Victorious Norman
knights pursuing the
fleeing English after the
Battle of Hastings; a scene
from the Bayeux Tapestry.

98

years.' Ordericus Vitalis, whose father was a Frenchman and although born himself in 1075 in England, lived nearly all his life in Normandy, which he deeply admired, wrote that:

> William in the fullness of his wrath ordered the corn and cattle, with the implements of husbandry and every sort of provisions, to be collected in heaps and set on fire until the whole was consumed and thus destroyed at once all that could serve for the support of life in the whole country lying beyond the Humber.

By such means, a famine was created by man and not by nature involving an 'innocent and unarmed population' in abject misery from which many died. The famine is estimated to have lasted for nine years, but was most relentless and grievous during the first three. Ordericus believed that 'such barbarous homicide' could not pass unpunished by the Almighty. It has been urged that 'the ravaging, to which William was driven in order to check his enemies, spared England the general anarchy which would have followed the destruction of Norman power'. Maybe, but the anarchy was surely the consequence of William's original invasion: after all, life in Anglo-Saxon England had not been all that bad. Assuredly, William's conquest was purchased at a terrible price.

ABOVE Norman soldiers burning down a house, while a Saxon woman and child escape; a scene from the Bayeux Tapestry.

OPPOSITE Warriors in Spain, from a copy, dating from 1220, of a tenth-century manuscript. The illustration shows archers, foot-soldiers armed with spears and cavalry. In the scene below, traitors are executed before the king.

Guthlac[?]

Guthlac' edificat
sibi capellam.

4 William and

the Church 1066-87

PREVIOUS PAGES
Two miniatures from the
Guthlac Roll at Crowland
Abbey, Lincolnshire.
Guthlac was an anchorite
who lived on the island
of Crowland in the Fens,
dying in 714. A monastery
grew up at Crowland,
which received his relics
in 1196, about the time
that this roll was executed.
Right: St Guthlac receiving
the tonsure at Repton
Abbey.
Left: St Guthlac
building an abbey.

RIGHT Edward the
Confessor, an illustration
from a fourteenth-century
manuscript.

DURING HIS REIGN King William took an extremely active part in the reorganisation of the English Church, although he went about it gradually. In Normandy, as Duke, William had been all-powerful in the government of the Church. Normandy contained one archbishopric (at Rouen) and six bishoprics. William not only chose the incumbents of all these sees but also appointed the abbots of monasteries. The men he selected were largely his friends and relations; thus, broadly speaking, the ecclesiastical and secular aristocracy in Normandy was a closely-knit group. It is true that after the death of one of his uncles and the disgrace of another, he appointed the saintly Maurilius as Archbishop of Rouen in 1055, but it has been suggested that by this time William had decided that a monastic revival was desirable in Normandy and deliberately gave the post to Maurilius for that reason. He was, however, an exception to the general rule. In fact, the Bishops of Coutances and Bayeux who came over with the Conqueror in 1066 were to spend much of their time carrying out administrative duties in England while it was being subdued.

It has sometimes been stated that before the Conquest, the Church in England was spiritually inferior to the Church in Normandy and that it was in many respects corrupt. The late Professor Brooke, writing in 1931, observed severely: 'The bishops were mostly uneducated, the lower clergy hopelessly ignorant.' That is rather surprising in view of the fact that Edward the Confessor was canonised and was reputed to have performed miracles in his lifetime. Certainly, Edward had been the effective head of the Church, which has been described as both royalist and nationalist. As God's vicar, Edward's right to make appointments to bishoprics and to the majority of monasteries was uncontested. How far Edward obtained monetary advantages in questionable. Both he and the Queen received gifts from time to time. But to accuse a saint of simony (that is, selling ecclesiastical offices) is shocking. It does, however, appear to be true that pluralism (the holding of more than one appointment), which has been consistently frowned upon by the Roman Church, was common in the England of Edward the Confessor. Still, pluralism is not easy to define; on some definitions, pluralism still exists in the Church of England. But undoubtedly Stigand was a case in point. When Edward

OVERLEAF Thirteenth-century miniatures of the miracles of Edward the Confessor. He was renowned for his piety and his healing touch and was reputed to have performed miracles during his lifetime.
RIGHT Above: Edward accuses Earl Godwin of the murder of the Atheling Alfred. Below: Godwin prepares to undergo trial by ordeal.
LEFT Above: Edward and Earl Leofric at Mass in Westminster Abbey see Jesus in the flesh. Below: Edward recovers from a pilgrim a ring which he had given to a beggar who was St John the Evangelist in disguise.

reluctantly replaced Robert of Jumièges as Archbishop of Canterbury by Stigand, he continued to hold the bishopric of Winchester and several abbeys as well. The Queen is said to have been aware of the scandalous state of the Church in England, and no one has argued that her husband was notably active or enlightened in his treatment of ecclesiastical questions. No great councils were summoned or reforms introduced during his reign. Still, he was a saint and he did build Westminster Abbey. Professor Loyn has written that 'modern opinion is much more favourably inclined towards the Old English Church and it is generally held now that culturally and in so far as contact with the papacy was concerned there were few sections of the universal church so healthy in essentials'.

The support of Archbishop Stigand was at first welcomed by King William, who kept him at his Court and listened to his advice. It was not until 1070 that Stigand was deposed by a council at which William was present and in which papal representatives took the lead. Stigand is sometimes described as a schismatic, presumably because he adhered to the wrong Pope at the wrong time. His supersession of Robert of Jumièges was considered improper, and he was excommunicated by no fewer than five Popes. When Aldred, Archbishop of York, died in September 1069, it left the excommunicate Stigand the only archbishop in England. William therefore assented to his deposition, pressed upon the King from Rome, and replaced him by Lanfranc, an Italian who had previously been persuaded to become Abbot of St Stephen's at Caen. Before Lanfranc's arrival in England, William had appointed Thomas, a canon of Bayeux, to the vacant archbishopric of York. But he left Thomas's consecration, as was customary, to Lanfranc.

Praises have been heaped upon Lanfranc by historians and biographers, although he never actually became a saint. He is described as a magnificent scholar who preferred the monastic life to the hurly-burly of Courts. Each step in his promotion he accepted with becoming reluctance. But he had always been on close terms with William, who, as has been noted, was particularly grateful to him for having procured the dispensation necessary for the Duke's canonical marriage to Matilda of Flanders. Once he came to England, Lanfranc proved himself to be a first-class administrator, whom William entrusted with

RIGHT St Benedict expounding his rule to the monks from an eleventh-century manuscript. The rule of St Benedict formed the basis of Western monasticism.

BELOW An illustration from *The Life of St Edward the King*, showing Edward the Confessor receiving petitions and letters.

a prominent part in the government of the kingdom when he himself was absent in Normandy or elsewhere. No doubt it was under the influence of Lanfranc that William carried out or approved the reorganisation of the Church in England. So far as is known, they always saw eye-to-eye. Indeed William of Poitiers waxes lyrical about the relationship between the two :

> William venerated him like a father, respected him like a master, cherished him as the equal of a brother or a son. It was to Lanfranc that he confided the direction of his soul, it was to him that he committed the duty of supervising by his watchfulness the ecclesiastical orders throughout the whole of Normandy. The vigilance of such a man, whose knowledge and holiness conferred upon him the right to the highest authority, secured nothing less than the best care for the Church.

In England Lanfranc was foremost in excommunicating rebels against his master and backed him up in resisting the claims of

BELOW The funeral procession of Edward the Confessor on its way to the recently-built Westminster Abbey – the most enduring monument to the reign of Edward the Confessor.

RIGHT Stigand,
Archbishop of Canterbury,
from the Bayeux
Tapestry. In 1070 the
Saxon Stigand was
deposed and replaced
by the Italian Lanfranc.

the Papacy to take a bigger part in ruling the English Church.

On Lanfranc's arrival in England he understandably regarded himself as responsible for the English Church and thought that it was his duty to reform it. When the English Church was founded by St Augustine, who had been sent over from Rome by Pope Gregory I in the sixth century to convert the Anglo-Saxons, his plan had been to set up one archbishopric in London and another in York, each archbishop having twelve bishops working under him. After St Augustine, himself the first archbishop, had arranged this, the archbishop of York was to become independent of Augustine's successors. But, as it happened, Kent was then the most civilised part of England and therefore Augustine became Archbishop of Canterbury. The Venerable Bede, whose history of the English Church is the principal authority for these early events, had little doubt about the primacy of the archbishop of Canterbury, who never in fact moved to London. Lanfranc satisfactorily concluded from his study of Bede and other authorities that he himself was the unquestioned head of the English Church. He has been pictured as 'sitting down with a Norman clerk beside him, working through the papal decrees and canons of the Councils [of the Church] in the book he had specially brought from Bec, and noting for future reference those passages which provided authority for the various sides of his work as metropolitan and primate'. Thus before he consecrated Thomas of Bayeux as Archbishop of York, he required a profession of obedience from him. Thomas gave it, though he did not see why any precedent should be established about the future dependence of York upon Canterbury. He also insisted that three out of the fifteen bishoprics that were in being when William came to England, those of Lichfield, Worcester and Dorchester (in Oxfordshire) properly belonged to his province.

In 1071, when both these archbishops journeyed to Rome to receive their *pallia*, Thomas reopened the question of the independence of York and of his claim to the three bishoprics. The Pope referred the tricky problem to a council in England and sent a legate to preside over its deliberations. Lanfranc produced an impressive display of evidence for his point of view including a series of papal letters which were unquestionably forged. It has been charitably assumed by English historians

that Lanfranc did not himself counterfeit the documents, partly on the ground that he was too scrupulous to do such a thing and partly because it has been felt that he hardly had the time to manufacture such forgeries. Forgeries then loomed large in the history of the Roman Church, and whether in fact Lanfranc arranged them himself or was innocently taken in by the monks of Canterbury, the fact remains that they were held to prove his case. It was decided that York was to be subject to Canterbury and Thomas was allowed to supervise only the bishop of Durham and such bishops as he might or might not find in Scotland.

Having cleared that difficulty out of the way, Lanfranc, with the approval of William, set about appointing as many Norman bishops as possible. The schismatic Stigand having been deposed, the bishopric of Winchester also fell vacant; so did the bishopric of North Elmham (subsequently situated at Thetford and afterwards at Norwich) which had been occupied by Stigand's brother. Aethelric of Selsey (which was to become the bishopric of Chichester) was also deposed, though he was brought to a conciliar meeting in a cart to answer questions about Anglo-Saxon law. Bishop Leofwine of Lichfield, being married with sons (marriage was an institution which did not command the approval of Lanfranc at any rate among his bishops and abbots), promptly took the prudent course of resigning his see. By the end of the reign, the only remaining English bishops were the ascetic Wulfstan of Worcester and Siward of Rochester, which was the smallest though also the richest of all the English sees. The other bishops were Norman or at any rate not English. Remigius of Fécamp received the bishopric of Dorchester as a reward for his political services; Bishop Osbern of Exeter was a brother of William's steward, William fitz Osbern, Earl of Hereford. The bishopric of Durham was given on the death of its English incumbent first to a clerk from Liège named Walcher, who in his dual capacity as Earl of Northumbria (he succeeded Robert of Commines) was killed by an infuriated mob in Gateshead in 1080, and then to William of Saint-Calais, in Maine.

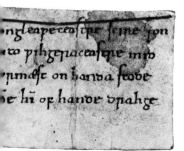

In order to strengthen and presumably to enrich the bishops, their sees were nearly all removed from truly rural to more populous areas. A precedent had been established during the

Church Architecture

Early Anglo-Saxon churches and monasteries were built of wood and covered with reeds. Later they were rebuilt in stone, small and simple, with a cruciform ground plan and triple arcade separating chancel and nave. After the Norman Conquest, the scale of churches increased and more complex Continental plans were adopted. However, older English traditions and tastes continued to assert themselves strongly.

BELOW LEFT The church of St Mary at Sompting near Worthing, which has a unique eleventh-century Anglo-Saxon tower with a 'Rhenish helm' spire.
BELOW RIGHT The tower of All Saints' Church, Earl's Barton, which has a tenth-century tower with characteristic Anglo-Saxon strip work.

LEFT Saxon windows from Holy Trinity Church, Deerhurst, in Gloucestershire.

RIGHT The church of St Mary the Virgin, Iffley, from the south-west. It is a magnificent example of late Norman architecture, built *c.* 1160–80. The façade is richly decorated with beak-head and zig-zag ornaments.

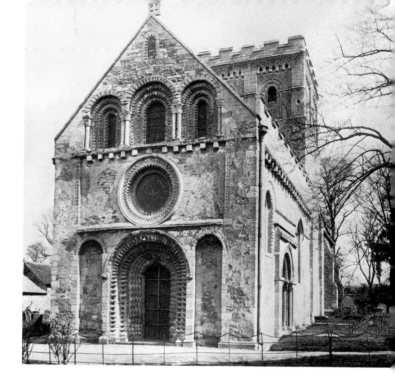

ABOVE LEFT AND RIGHT
Exterior and interior of the round church of the Holy Sepulchre, Cambridge, an unusual example of Norman church architecture, built *c.* 1130.

reign of Edward the Confessor when the see of Crediton was moved to Exeter. Lichfield was transferred to Chester, Sherborne to Salisbury and Dorchester to Lincoln. The plan for placing centres of sees in urban districts and a scheme of precedence for the bishops were decided upon at the second of Lanfranc's ecclesiastical councils, which met in London during 1075. William was away in Normandy at the time, but his authorisation was obtained. It also happened that in 1067 Maurilius, the devout Archbishop of Rouen, died and was replaced by John of Avranches, who was a cadet of the Norman ducal house. Thus by the 1070s nearly all the bishops both in England and in Normandy were friends or relations of William. He therefore had no reason to expect any problems over them, although he did eventually feel obliged to imprison his half-brother, the Bishop of Bayeux.

The abbots of the thirty-five Benedictine houses which existed in England in 1066 were also subjected to the same process of *Gleichstaltung*. William suspected that many of the abbots were involved in a political resistance movement. They were therefore extruded and reliable men from Normandy or elsewhere in France were substituted. To give one instance, quoted by Ordericus Vitalis, the Abbot of Croyland happened to be a friend of Earl Waltheof, who had his head cut off for treason : the Abbot, 'being English-born and therefore disliked by the Normans, being accused by his rivals, was deposed by Archbishop Lanfranc and sent into confinement at Glastonbury'.

As to the Church as a whole, William's policy according to Eadmer, a chronicler who wrote in the twelfth century, was 'to sustain in England the same usages and laws which he and his ancestors were wont to observe in Normandy'. Following the precedent set in Normandy, both bishops and abbots were required to provide armed and mounted knights for the service of the King when he required them: for example, the see of Winchester and the abbey of Peterborough had each (according to later records) to furnish sixty knights.

Nevertheless it is generally admitted that the calibre of the foreign monks was high and that the Norman conquerors contributed quite generously to the expansion of monastic life in England. William himself had an abbey, first called Holy Trinity, built on the site of his victory at Hastings, later to

OPPOSITE A page from a thirteenth-century manuscript showing, in the right margin, a drawing of Battle Abbey, founded by William on the site of the Battle of Hastings to commemorate his victory. The initial drawing shows the coronation of William, which can be seen in greater detail on page 48.

...nativitatis die ab aldredo ebor archiepo regni suscepit diadema. Timuit .n. hoc mini osecratoris a frigando cant archiepo iuscape q no legitime occupauit illi excellentiam dignitatis. lice de uire antiq ad illā ecclam illā sollempnitas spectare cuplit. dein ho magus a magnatibz cū fidelitatis iuramiro obsidibz q receptis i regno ofirmauit. onibz quoz dispositis. z castellis, puisa ministris ipositis. ad normaniam cū obsidibz anglie z thesauris impacabilibz nauigauit. Quibz in cariatis z sub salua custodia deputatis. ad angliā demu remeauit. Ubi cōmilitoibz suis normannis q in bello hastingensi pru seuit subiugauit. cras angloz z possiones ipis expulsis successiue manu tribut afflu erit. z modicis illo q eis remanserat fra iam de rege tyrani sub iugo detrusit seruitute. Et cū se uidet in sullim eleua tu. z fastu regni ofirmatū. manū uirium subito e cōmutatus. Nobiles ire qs antiq sanguis ab antiq sūmaciat p dolor ocul cando. Uū nobiliores de regno indignati qdam ad rege scotoz malcolinū ofugerut. Alii malentes uitā infelice finuiare. qz ser uirut insoluta subire. loca deserta z nemo rosa ptetes. Ubiq uitā feralem ducentes. noz manius cessisse princetes. z dolore uehemi corde intrinsecus tacti seuo que potertit occul tas insidias z dāpna pnauert. Uidetes q pfs sua instinuioz z setuiute tenuentes. re cesserut ab anglia comites geriosi. eadwni z moretard fres. mercher z wetrpls nobiles cū epis z clias z alus multis quos longū e ptime noiarim. Q onīs ad rege scotoz malcolinū fugientes ab ip honouifice sūt recepti. Sic z eadgarus ethcling de regno angloz heres legittim' certiens res pūte in...

dia distraha z pmutari accusa naui cum agitha matre sua z sororibz margareta z xpi na. Thuringiā iu namis fuar. reiti conaliī s tempestate subora compulsus e i scocia applicat. Hac quoq occone actū fuit ut mar gareta regi malcolino nupta traderet. Cui uira laudabilem z more pciosam liber spiali me editus. insidinat cuiderit. Sorol at eius cristina scimonial b̄dicat celesti sposo p cuo copulata. Nam sūt deniq regine mar garet sex filii z due filie. quoz res eadgarus salu. dauid z alexander uū genius siu nobili tat reges fuerūt. Er quibz regib; anglie no bilitas appris p normannos expulsa fimbz ad regis eet deuolura scotoz. Quare willi rex conserat e mun rex Willi z coronatus die natiuitatis duice fr̄ ij. ab alvredo ebor archiepo. qz stigand cant archiepe raq ssmarie ab alexandro pp suspirius erat. Vacabit at tuc tpus ecca Londomie.

Dec iū Willis exultans de iuctoria redit laude deo. Construit irx albariam. qm appla uit p bello i cōmisso. belli. In q i sprū do gla tias z graz actio p uictoria ospitata soluet. Secno z p idem mortus exepcue a scis monachis ibi ofituris cū sauraibz hostibz cō reddet. ipsumq eccam possibz z libariis dotarā z diuiā cōmisit patronatui z tu tele regij q p eū fouerit in anglia regnatui.

Matildis uxor regis willi osceruit in re gina die pentechosten ab alveredo ebor archiepo. v. kl' aprilis. Hoc i anno natr regi willo in anglia filii. z uocare est henric. Nam pmogeniti ei. W. rufus z robrus i normā nia nati sūt ante q pr cor anglie subiugauer. Int duo festa t̄ marie i autūpno uenerut duo filii swani de dacia cū .ccc. nauibz i an glia ut ipam hostiliter expugnaret. z Willm rege ul caperit ul ab anglia effugaret. Quoz aduentu cū diuulgett eet exeritt ut obuiam comites z barones z nobiles tir. oppressi a normannoz importabili supbia z sedus ferientes cū ip addiri sūt exeitui dam ut regē w. ofundent. S; rex w. prudent sim iudens pctm imuere humiliauit se illis cōpresens elatione suoz normanoz. Et sic reuocatis multis angloz nobilibz federe cauel cū oibz ofirmato. eboraci ubi fuit da noz receptaclm potenr cū i inuentis expug nauit. z multa milia hōim occidit ibicem.

Cō. lxix.
duo filii swam
ueniūt i ōgliā

become known as Battle Abbey. William of Warenne, a Norman nobleman, who fought with the Conqueror at Hastings, founded a Cistercian priory at Lewes, which thus became one of the first 'white-monk' houses in England. The 'black-monk' houses were increased in size, one or two small houses being created through Norman gifts. The new bishops under the leadership of Lanfranc decided to add to the number of monastic cathedrals; there were four at the beginning of the reign, including Canterbury, which was rebuilt, and seven at the end of it. The Normans were also mainly responsible for establishing archdeacons as the administrative agents of the bishops. A council of 1072 ordered all bishops to appoint archdeacons.

In Anglo-Saxon England, besides the churches of the archbishops and bishops which were established in their sees, such as Christ Church at Canterbury, there had developed a number of missionary, mother churches or minsters – in east Kent, for example, there were four, including one at Maidstone. Minsters were manned by groups of canons who served several villages. Baptisms usually took place in these old minsters, or at any rate they were the channel for the supply of holy oil for baptism known as chrism. In the reign of William, the minsters were in a state of decay or had been given to monasteries. On the other hand, the parish organisation apparently received a stimulus from the Norman Conquest. A parish was a lesser church, usually established in a manor with a permanent priest and a graveyard. The manorial lords appointed the priests and sometimes dismissed them. Yet fifteen years before the Conquest, an English bishop boasted in Rome of the great number of churches and bells in England. Probably the new secular aristocracy encouraged the building of manorial churches or village churches for the good of their souls and also the advantage of their pockets, for most lords drew rents from their churches. But much of the money for building churches came from the ecclesiastical lords, and their inclination was to construct cathedrals or larger churches as status symbols.

An English chronicler, William of Malmesbury, writing about seventy years after the Conquest said that the Normans

> ... after their coming to England revived the rule of religion which had there grown lifeless. You might see churches rise in every

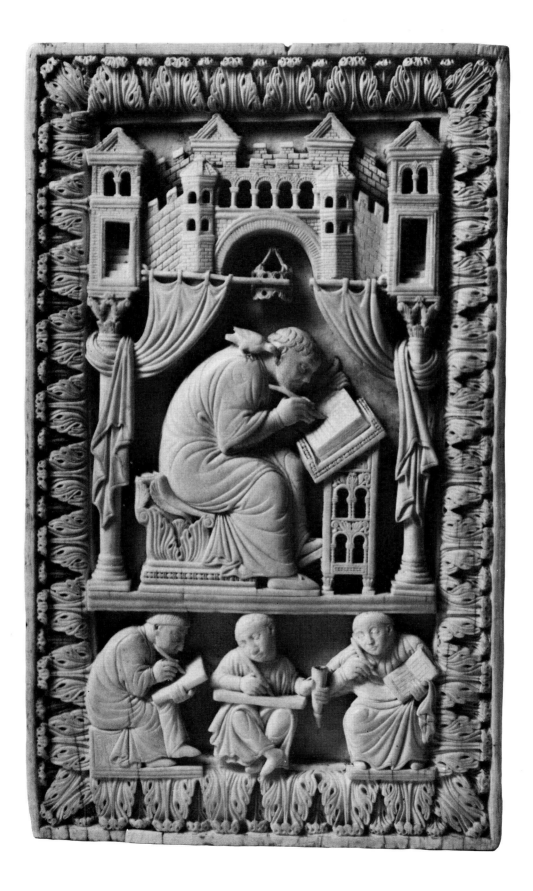

village, or in the towns and cities; monasteries built after a style unknown before: you could watch the country flourishing with renewed religious observance: each wealthy man counted the day lost in which he had neglected some outstanding benefaction.

One imagines that this chronicler, who, after all, was not a contemporary witness of what happened, exaggerated, as chroniclers usually did.

Lanfranc held three important councils in 1072, 1075 and 1076. The first insisted that all bishops should have archdeacons; the second concentrated on the organisation of the bishops and bishoprics; the last was chiefly devoted to the question of celibacy and to protecting the status of parish priests.

Lanfranc was an enthusiast for clerical celibacy. That is why he threw the weight of his influence behind the expansion of monasteries and monks (though not apparently of nunneries). The difficulty was not only that several bishops and canons were married, but so also were the majority of parish priests. Indeed, Pope Gregory I had permitted English clerics in minor orders, that is to say below the rank of sub-deacon, to marry. It was all very well to lay down stringent rules upon the subject, to say that in future no priest might take a wife, though priests already married might keep their wives, but the question remained how a rule of celibacy could be enforced in practice. If the priests did not officially have wives, then they very often had mistresses or house-keepers. The fact is that, during the Middle Ages in England, few celibate priests were to be discovered outside the more strictly controlled monasteries.

Even in Normandy, the maintenance of clerical celibacy did not prove at all easy. Archbishop John of Rouen, so Ordericus Vitalis informs us, took severe measures to separate incontinent priests from their concubines; but 'when in a synod [in 1072] he prohibited their intercourse under the pain of excommunication, he was assailed with stones, and after fleeing from the church, he intoned with a loud voice the verse [from the Psalms]: "O God, the heathen are come into their inheritance."'

The difficulty over laying down all these fresh rules about the organisation of the English Church, including the protection of the property and morals of parish priests, was invariably how to impose a code of discipline. In Anglo-Saxon England, spiritual questions might come before the county courts and as

LEFT An ivory carving, c. 980, showing monks at work writing and illuminating Bibles, missals and psalters.

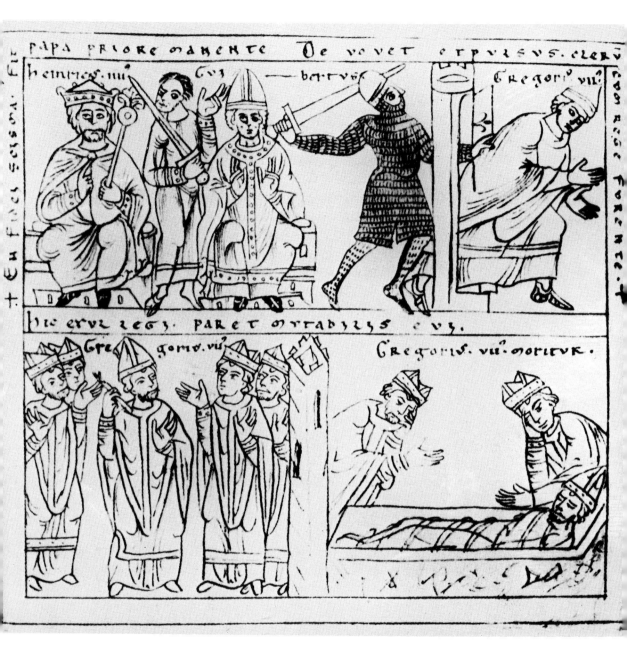

Scenes from the life of Gregory VII, Pope from 1073 to 1085. In 1080 the Council of Brixen deposed Gregory and pronounced Archbishop Guibert of Ravenna his successor. The scene above shows the German Emperor, Henry IV, with the new Pope, enthroned as Clement III; on the right, Gregory VII is driven into exile by the Emperor's soldiers. Below, Gregory is shown with his clergy, and, on the right, on his deathbed.

124

the local bishop generally served in these courts, questions of Church discipline might naturally be settled by him. But the average peasant did not undertake the arduous journey to the county court, but went to the hundred courts (the hundred being a subdivision of the county). Thus it was the hundred courts which must have dealt with day-to-day spiritual quest-ions. In 1072, however, William published a decree with-drawing ecclesiastical cases from the hundred courts and empowering the bishops or their archdeacons to set up their own courts to determine matters 'according to the canons and episcopal laws'. The separation of lay and ecclesiastical justice was, in fact, a common practice outside England. The forma-tion of these spiritual courts, which were to proliferate, became a virulent source of controversy between the future kings and their archbishops of Canterbury. Evidently William did not anticipate that, possibly on account of the close and happy co-operation between Archbishop Lanfranc and himself.

The relationship between the King and the Papacy was never entirely clear or satisfactory. Both in Normandy and in Eng-land, William was jealous of his independence and guarded his right to appoint all bishops and abbots and to authorise the decrees promulgated by ecclesiastical councils. 'The idea of a centralised Church directly controlled in all its parts by the Pope' was, according to Professor Brooke, 'from every point of view distasteful to him'. He did not mind the Popes con-firming his appointees, for example, by giving the archbishops their *pallia*. He was also prepared to refer knotty questions of Canon Law to the authority of Rome and he welcomed the assistance of papal legates in getting rid of English bishops and abbots whom he disliked or distrusted. But he would never acknowledge the right of the Pope spontaneously to interfere with the government of the English Church. He would not permit anyone to receive letters from the Pope unless he saw them first, or allow anyone to go to Rome without his leave. He much resented Leo IX's prohibition of his marriage and in effect he ignored it.

On the other hand, William undoubtedly put himself under a moral obligation to the Papacy when he secured the judgment of Alexander II, prompted by his archdeacon Hildebrand, that he was the legitimate heir to the English throne and might fight

Norman Cathedrals

In every branch of art except architecture, the Norman Conquest resulted, for a while at least, in a decline from the achievements of the Anglo-Saxon period. But the Normans were the greatest builders of their time, and their achievements can be seen not only in Normandy and England but in Apulia and Sicily as well. There are some magnificent survivals of this late phase of Romanesque architecture in England, although none of them have escaped substantial alterations.

BELOW LEFT The north transept of St Alban's Cathedral, the oldest example of Norman cathedral architecture in England. There had been a Benedictine abbey on its site since 793, but the church was entirely rebuilt between 1077 and 1115 by Paul de Caen and Richard d'Aubeney, the first two Norman abbots.
BELOW RIGHT Norman arches in the north transept of Winchester Cathedral, built between 1079 and 1093 from limestone brought from the Isle of Wight.

Durham Cathedral is the masterpiece of
Romanesque architecture in England. Begun
towards the end of William's reign, the whole
church, with the exception of the towers,
was completed within only forty years.
RIGHT The north portal of Durham
Cathedral. On the door is a magnificent piece
of Romanesque metalwork – a bronze
'sanctuary' knocker.
BELOW The impressive nave of Durham
Cathedral, looking east. At the vault of the nave
there was a great innovation; the transverse
arches, for the first time, were pointed.

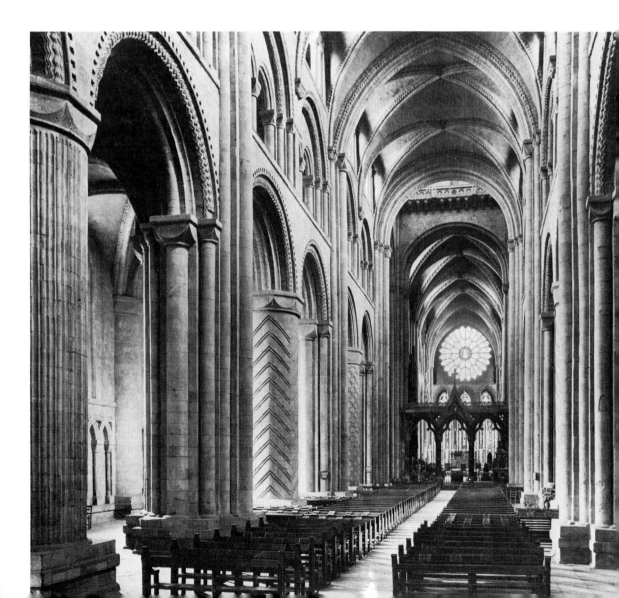

for his inheritance under the papal banner. But when Hildebrand himself became Pope in 1073, he was highly indignant that William had prevented archbishops and bishops from visiting Rome when they wished to do so. William then made an effort to conciliate Gregory VII, but it merely provoked the claim from Gregory that William should do fealty to him for his kingdom. As the demand was conveyed verbally to the King by one of the Pope's legates in 1080, it is not known with certainty upon what grounds Gregory based his claim. They may have been historical, going back to the time of St Augustine; they may have been connected with the traditional payment of 'Peter's Pence', an annual tribute by the kingdom to the Papacy; or they may have been related to the papal support granted to Duke William in 1066. Whatever the arguments put forward in fact were, the Pope's demand or request received a sharp answer from William. He replied: 'I have not consented to pay fealty, nor will I now because I never promised it, nor do I find that my predecessors ever paid it to your predecessors.' When, not long afterwards, owing to his dispute with the Emperor Henry IV, Gregory VII was chased from Rome, and an anti-Pope, Clement III, put there in his place, William and Lanfranc reckoned that henceforward they had been given a free hand. In the words of Professor Brooke, William 'did not decide between the two Popes himself, nor did he allow any of his subjects to decide for themselves. This removed any question of papal authority at all.'

William, we are assured by contemporary chroniclers and by historians expert in the subject, was a sincere and pious Christian justly renowned for his reforming zeal. He dedicated a considerable part of his busy life to ecclesiastical affairs. Not only did he select all the bishops and discover in Lanfranc an archbishop of zeal and distinction, but he himself was the sole link between the Churches in England and Normandy. He supervised the ecclesiastical councils which met in both his kingdom and his duchy, and was therefore an active co-ordinating agent, who assumed the responsibility for the welfare and reform of the Church throughout his dominions. He was also determined that discipline should be firmly exercised in the Church and, to some extent at least, he carried out something approaching revolutionary changes in England. Professor Barlow, always a realist, is perhaps less enthusiastic over what William did for the English Church than some of William's other biographers. He uses the word 'adroit' about the King's handling of the Church as a whole and suggests that some of his more imaginative schemes, especially in relation to the monasteries, failed altogether.

One policy that William consistently followed, if at first slowly, was that of filling all the principal offices of the English Church with foreigners, mainly Normans. By the end of the reign only one or two bishops of Anglo-Saxon origin remained and he would never allow Englishmen to be promoted abbots; again, nearly all the new abbots came to England from Normandy (not from Cluny, the model monastery in Burgundy). As to the bishops, Edward the Confessor himself had set an example when he had chosen Robert of Jumièges as Archbishop of Canterbury. Nothing is really known about the attitude of the English clergy as a whole to their new foreign masters, but it can hardly have been exactly cordial. Undoubtedly some of the imports were impressively pious. We have had preserved for us at some length the story of a venerable monk whom the King summoned from Normandy to offer him promotion in England. This redoubtable cleric asked William for permission to return to Normandy, saying 'I abandon the rich plunder of England as so much trash to men of the world. I prefer the free poverty of Christ. . . .' William and everyone else were astonished.

'I abandon the rich plunder of England'

But most of the bishops whom William selected were less altruistic and were, like himself, extremely capable administrators. No doubt they were devout according to their lights, and it may even be urged that what is required in a bishop is administrative capacity as much as deeply-felt Christianity. It may also be observed that in the eleventh century Christian administrators were interchangeable throughout western Europe, all of them using dog Latin as their language, just as a class of international civil servants exists throughout western Europe today who speak much the same kind of language in the technical sense.

One of the achievements of the Normans, because of the extent of their conquests, was to help spread a unified Canon Law, particularly in England. Furthermore, even an Anglo-

The consecration of the
third abbey church at
Cluny by Pope Urban in
1095. The Pope stands
on the left of the altar
and Abbot Hugh on the
right. This Benedictine
monastery in Burgundy
was founded in 910, and
soon, as a result of a series
of energetic and able
abbots who devoted
themselves to reform,
came to have a great
influence on European
civilisation. Close links
were established with
reformed monasteries in
England, Italy, Spain and
Germany, as well as France,
and during the abbacy of
St Hugh, the Cluniac
Order was granted official
recognition by Urban II.
At the height of its
popularity, in the early
twelfth century, the
Cluniac Order consisted
of nearly 15,000
monasteries.

130

regi uel principi curam ipsius
tutelamq; commendauit. nisi
deo et beato Petro eiusq; uica
rus. romanis scilicet pontificib'
Auoꝶ numero uel ordini diuina
me dignatio licet indignum as
sociauit. me olim monachum
prioremq; monasterii huius. sub
domno ac uenerabili hugone

hugo

Anglo-Norman ivory head of a tall cross, dating from the twelfth century, from Le Mans.

Saxon chronicler praises what William did for monasticism in England (though here no doubt Lanfranc also made a major contribution). The Peterborough chronicler writes of William:

> Though stern beyond measure to those who opposed his will, he was kind to those good men who loved God. On the very spot where God granted him the conquest of England he caused a great abbey to be built; and he settled monks in it and richly endowed it. During his reign was [re]built the great cathedral at Canterbury and many another throughout all England. The land was filled with monks living their lives after the rule of St Benedict. Such was the state of religion in his time that every man who wished to, whatever considerations there might have been with regard to their rank, could follow the profession of monk.

Thus it might be said that both the Church in England and that in Normandy benefited from William's reign over England. The Church in Normandy was enriched by the wealth seized by the conquerors; for example, William's half-brother Odo was able as Earl of Kent to enhance his bishopric at Bayeux with spoils lifted from England. Both the Norman bishoprics and monasteries were granted, or at any rate received, lands in a variety of English shires.

Two problems which were to harrass later English kings, the

132

question of lay investiture of bishops and the conflict between the secular and church courts when a criminal who could claim 'benefit of clergy' might get off without being subjected to the severest penalties, did not arise during the reign of William I. Indeed it might be said that he created them and that the only reason why they did not develop more rapidly was because of the contest that began between Popes and anti-Popes during the later part of the reign. Professor Barlow notes that William 'can hardly have been without misgivings about the future'. Still, on balance, one may say that King William conferred some advantages on the English Church: it became administratively tidy, if that is what people like to see.

5 The Introduction of Feudalism 1066-87

I IT USED TO BE SAID that William introduced 'feudalism' from Normandy into England. By feudalism is meant the system whereby a tenant or 'vassal' held land from his superior or 'lord' in return for providing him with specific services, of which the most important were military services, whenever they were required. This was termed holding land as a 'fief' or 'in fee' and became the characteristic method of land tenure in much of early medieval Europe. Gradually a number of other obligations between a vassal and his lord grew up, which were called feudal 'incidents', such as for example, the 'relief', which was the payment made to his lord by a tenant whenever a previous tenant had died. The feudal method of land tenure is really less complicated than it sounds. It was basically a particular way of paying rent and in the course of time nearly all feudal services or incidents were converted or 'commuted' into money payments.

What in fact happened in England during the reign of William was that much of the land in the kingdom was confiscated from the English nobility and granted by the monarch to Normans and other Frenchmen or to Flemings. The principle was asserted that all land belonged to the King. But in fact by the end of his reign, William owned directly only between one sixth and one seventh net of the landed income of the country, whereas a small group comprised mainly of Norman families – the King's tenants-in-chief – acquired about half the territorial wealth of the conquered kingdom. In 1086, only two Englishmen still retained large estates held directly from the King. The Norman conquerors, on the other hand, not only owned a great deal of land in England, granted to them in return for their services to the King, but also kept and sometimes increased the lands they had in Normandy. Most of these very rich families were interlinked and many of them were related to William himself. It was the introduction of this new aristocracy – or plutocracy – which is the fundamental political, social and economic fact that was established by the Norman Conquest of England.

The units King William created in England for his principal followers were known as 'honours' – an honour normally consisted of lands scattered through many English shires. The honour would have a centre (in Latin *caput*), generally a castle

where the great lord lived and from which he governed his many estates. William founded 170 honours in England. The smaller territorial unit or estate, which varied considerably in size, was called by the Normans a manor; and one great lord might hold many manors dispersed all over the country. These manors he would either have cultivated himself, in which case it was known as his 'demesne' land or let to tenants in return for rent and services. Every man had a master, from the tenants-in-chief down to the ordinary 'villans' or smallholders and humble cottagers.

It was once thought that King William deliberately adopted the policy of dispersing or scattering the manors of his tenants-in-chief so as to prevent any of them becoming so territorially powerful that they could threaten his own supremacy. This theory has been abandoned; modern research has tended to suggest that the distribution of lands belonging to the great

ABOVE LEFT The keep of Arundel Castle, typical of the Norman castles raised by William's barons from which to control the surrounding countryside. Arundel was awarded to Roger of Montgomery, whose earldom included part of Sussex.

ABOVE RIGHT Norman soldiers building a fortress – probably a wooden stockade on a mound, a scene from the Bayeux Tapestry.

magnates – the holders of the 'honours' – may have been related to the earlier territorial associations or arrangements which existed in Normandy; alternatively large estates confiscated by William could already have consisted of landholdings scattered in Anglo-Saxon times and thus the same pattern was preserved. William did, however, grant compact blocks of territory at strategic points throughout the kingdom, not only on the borders of Wales and Scotland, where his earls were expected to maintain security, but also in coastal areas where an enemy might disembark. Clearly the procedure was modelled on the *comtés* of Normandy. In time William came to suspect the loyalty of the English secular lords, just as much as he did that of the English bishops and abbots. Thus for one reason or another he deprived them of their possessions and gave them to men whom he believed he could trust and who paid for them with military services or in a few cases provided 'money fiefs' which would enable him to call up a potent army whenever he needed it.

The King's tenants-in-chief, then, came to hold their lands in return for the provision of knights' services. Each lord of an honour would undertake to furnish the King with a specified number of mounted and armed knights – that is to say cavalry-men – whenever he wanted them for a period of military duty either abroad or at home. In England, these knights might be called up to go on campaign against the Welsh or the Scots or to repress rebellions, or again they might be required to keep guard in castles owned by the King. In this way it has been estimated that William had at his disposal five thousand knights. The knights were of two kinds. There were household knights, who lived with and immediately served their honorial lord, riding with him as he made his progresses over his vast estates, and there were 'enfeoffed knights', who were given lands in return for military services when they were needed and other regular payments of one kind or another. The process whereby the King's tenants-in-chief created knights both under obligation to them and available for royal duties was called sub-infeudation. Most great tenants-in-chief had a larger number of knights in their service than they were required to furnish to the King. But the maintenance of knights was a substantial item in a lord's expenditure, even if a knight was not so skilfully trained and equipped and was far less glamorous than he became in later European history. Still, the services of knights added to the political effectiveness of a nobleman in Norman times and thereby increased his power and influence.

The King's object in granting land in return for knights' service was in order that he might be able to collect properly equipped cavalrymen whenever he needed them. But these knights formed only a part of his armies. In fact the King often hired mercenaries – professional soldiers, many of whom had, for example, fought at Hastings – and these he paid for out of the proceeds of taxation. In the reign of Edward the Confessor and earlier in English history, when a king wanted money to raise troops to fight Scandinavian invaders or for other purposes, he collected a general tax or 'geld'. The geld was assessed according to the amount of arable land owned in villages or groups of villages. The commonest unit of assessment was known as the 'hide' or normal peasant holding. Two shillings a hide was the usual annual rate of assessment. The total amount of money needed was determined by the county courts and a quota assigned to each hundred. William did not neglect to make use of this old, if unpopular, English custom and towards the end of his reign, when he was involved in widespread warfare on the European mainland, he demanded and obtained heavy gelds. Finally, in times of crisis when the kingdom was menaced with invasion from abroad or rebellion at home, the King could call up all men capable of bearing arms, militiamen who were known in Anglo-Saxon days as the 'fyrd'. As has been observed, King Harold II called up the local fyrds during his campaigns in 1066. But the fyrd was not a very efficient force and was seldom employed by William.

The King therefore made the utmost use of the institutions which he found in a kingdom richer and more populous than the duchy of Normandy. It has been estimated that the population of England was well over a million and that the fyrd might have consisted of ten thousand men, the heads of families. Thus William could mobilise a formidable army. In some ways England was more advanced than Normandy and in other ways less so. For instance, it appears that the Saxon thegn, a man of noble birth and generally of adequate means, was a less experienced soldier than a Norman knight and did not usually fight

Norman knights on their way to battle, from
the Bayeux Tapestry. The provision by the
tenants-in-chief of knights' service to
the King in return for grants of land, was
the basis of feudalism.

AD PRO

from horseback. On the other hand, thegns were frequently granted charters under the auspices of the Church which allowed them to hold land free from the burdens required by the ordinary folk law. This 'book-land', as it was called, which was purchased by thegns, may well have been paid for by the promise of military services. It was therefore not unlike benefices granted by William or his tenants-in-chief to their vassals. The services required by the English King or by an English magnate who had granted a 'book' to a thegn might include such duties as standing guard, repairing fortresses or equipping ships. (It has even been suggested that the resources of five hides of land produced a warrior for the fyrd, but the evidence for that is extremely debatable.) Therefore, though similarities may be detected between the kind of duties performed by a thegn in return for his 'book' or charter and those performed by a knight in return for a Norman benefice, those duties related to a thegn's status rather than his tenure. Thus the idea that any elaborate 'feudal system' was already in existence when the Normans conquered England has not been proved.

In any case it may well be contended that the whole concept of 'feudalism' as expounded in the seventeenth century and as discussed during the nineteenth century exaggerated the importance of the armed knight in medieval warfare. Certainly, as can be seen from a close analysis of the Battle of Hastings, it was not the mounted knights who were by any means mainly responsible for William's victory. And when later William enlisted English soldiers to fight in his wars in Normandy and neighbouring duchies or counties they were principally infantry. After all, pitched battles, like that at Hastings, were a rarity: warfare consisted largely in the attack, defence or relief of castles for which cavalry was not at all essential. Cavalry was used for skirmishes, reconnaissance or protecting the movements of the infantry. The soldiers of fortune or mercenaries employed by William might have moved on horseback, but, like Harold's housecarls, they generally fought on foot. They had no desire to risk their expensive horses being killed in attacking fortified towns.

Military strategy therefore revolved around the swapping of castles as upon a chess board or in laying waste the countryside so that castle garrisons or the inhabitants of towns were isolated

Norman bowmen from the Bayeux Tapestry. Norman archers contributed significantly to the victory at Hastings. The usual form of bow at this period was the cross-bow – the long-bow did not become popular in England until the thirteenth century.

and could be starved out. In the actual siege of castles much play-acting must have taken place. For the garrisons preferred to surrender rather than to have their buildings put to the sack or burned to the ground. Blockades, as that of Brionne, might last for months on end. One would not say that early medieval warfare was particularly gentlemanly in character, but the rules of the game were recognised by both sides and were seldom violated. So while the armoured knight may have been the *raison d'être* of the 'feudal system' he can have played only a limited and chiefly defensive part in warfare.

May it be argued that the feudal system was introduced from Normandy? Again, this does not appear to have been the fact, although, as has been remarked, some Norman monasteries are said to have held land from the Duke in return for the provision of knights' service. The essential point was that the wholesale confiscation of English landed estates enabled William, who was in need of a good army, to recruit one through dependent tenure. William was a splendid organiser. The conquest of England gave him the opportunity to establish a general system of knights' service to man his army and castles, but this service

IS: PVG NANT: CONTRA

Normans besieging the castle of Dinant, from the Bayeux Tapestry. Since the castle was such a vital element of warfare and conquest, much of medieval fighting took the form of sieges.

was probably not based on a specific assessment of property and may have varied from case to case. Professor Barlow stresses that 'the logic and symmetry of Anglo-Norman feudalism were due to its imposition on a conquered country by a strong king', while Professor Douglas has written 'when all qualifications have been made, there can be no question that the destruction of one aristocracy in England and the substitution of another holding its lands by military tenure involved a revolutionary change'. In other words, King William neither inherited 'the feudal system' from his Anglo-Saxon predecessors nor did he bring it over as part of his luggage from Rouen. The case for continuity is not generally accepted. What William did was to take a unique opportunity to demand extensive military duties from his nobility. Historians, who know what was going to happen later in English history, can well feel that this particular method of forming the core of a royal army was not going to last very long nor to prove notably efficient. Furthermore, the process of subinfeudation enabled the great men of the kingdom to have private armies – and also, as it proved, private castles – at their disposal. In the reign of a weak king, like Stephen or an unfortunate king like John the result was to be anarchy.

Let us now turn to the Domesday Survey. This was the background. In 1086 King Canute IV of Denmark, whose father King Swein had invaded England in 1070 but had been induced to withdraw on being granted favourable terms by King William, and who himself had in 1075 been invited over to England by the three rebellious earls, now decided to revive his family's claim to the English throne, which his immediate predecessor and elder brother, Harold, had allowed to lapse. Canute gathered a large fleet, but in fact the invasion never took place and in the autumn the Danish ships dispersed. William was sufficiently alarmed to summon over from France a substantial army of mercenaries, which showed incidentally that neither his knights nor the English fyrd were thought by him capable of providing enough military protection for his kingdom. These mercenaries had to be paid for and undoubtedly an economic slump must have occurred at about that time; after all, it would scarcely have been surprising if an economic depression had not been in progress in view of the drastic shifts in the landed wealth of England that were then taking place. At any rate, around Christmas 1085 William held Court at Gloucester and took counsel with his principal advisers and household officers: this was the nucleus of what came to be known as the *Curia Regis*, which was to become the central administrative organ of the kingdom. It was decided to institute a thorough investigation into the wealth of the entire country. The Peterborough Chronicler relates that after having exhaustive discussion about how the land was peopled 'and with what sort of men', King William:

> ... sent his men all over England into every shire to ascertain how many hundreds of hides of land there were in each shire and how much land and livestock the King himself owned in the country

147

RE: ... LIST

and what annual dues were lawfully his from each shire. He also had it recorded how much land his archbishops had, and his diocesan bishops, his abbots and his earls and . . . what or how much each man, who was a landholder here in England, had in land and in livestock, and how much money it was worth. So very thoroughly did he have the inquiry carried out that there was not a single hide nor one virgate [thirty acres, a fraction, sometimes a quarter, of a hide] not even – it is shameful to record it but it did not seem shameful to him to do it – one ox or one cow or pig which escaped notice in his survey.

The survey was not a mere 'geld book', aiming to inform the King's agents how much they could collect in the form of land taxes. In any case, as Professor Galbraith pointed out, geld was

Norman soldiers loading arms and supplies on to their boats: they include hauberks (suits of mail), spears, swords, helmets, barrels of wine and water. and sacks of flour.

PORTANT:ARMAS: ADNAVES: ET HIC TRAHVNT:CARRVM CVM VINO:ET ARM IS:

just one and not necessarily the most profitable of many royal taxes or customs levied annually. What took place was in fact a full-scale inquiry into the actual and potential wealth and income of the kingdom.

Even more remarkable than the scope of the survey is the speed and efficiency with which it was carried out. The kingdom was divided into seven circuits; impartial commissioners summoned to each county court landholders and manorial tenants but not, as used to be said, 'juries' from every village in every hundred to answer their questions. On the basis of information already known or collected at the sittings of the courts, called 'sworn inquests', it was aimed to describe not only what land and other property, such as ox teams and slaves, were

149

In Burgo MALMESBERIE habet rex .xxvi. masuras hospitatas. 7 xx.v. masuras in qib3 fed dom9 q[ue] n[on] reddunt geld3 pluq[uam] uasta t[er]ra. Una quaq; haru[m] masuraru[m] redd. x. den. de gablo. hoc e[st] simul .xl.iii. sol. 7 vi. den. 7 seruitiu[m] reddu[n]t.

De feudo epi baiocsis. e[st] ibi dimidia masura uasta. q[ue] nulli. Abb malmesbie h[abe]t .iii. m[a]s[u]ras. 7 fore3 burg. xx. colcez q[ui] geld[an]t cu[m] burgsib3. Abb Glastingbiens h[abe]t .ii. masur. Eduuardo .iii. masur. Radulf de mortem .i. 7 dim3. Durand de Glouuec. .i. 7 dim3. Wills de ow .i. Hunfrid de insula .i. Osb[er]n9 Gisard .i. Aluered de Merleb3. dim3 mas uasta. Goisfrid similit. Iouis .i. q[ua]rta parte uni3 mas. Drogo. f. ponz. dim3. Nigel Ex[on?] .i. Rog de berchelai .i. mas de firma regis. 7 b[er]nius .i. simile de firma regis. q[uam] in cauere accep. h[a]e due3 nulla[m] seruitute[m] reddu[n]t.

Rex h[abe]t una[m] uasta[m] masuram de t[er]ra qua[m] Azor tenuit.

Hic Annotantur Tenentes Terras In Wiltescire.

.i. Rex Willelmus.	.xxxvi. Walscanus de Dowai.
.ii. Eps Wintoniensis.	.xxxvii. Walelen uenator.
.iii. Eps Sarisberiensis.	.xxxviii. Willelm filius Widonis.
.iiii. Eps Baiocensis.	.xxxix. Henricus de Fereres.
.v. Eps Constantiensis.	.xl. Ricard filius Gisleberti.
.vi. Eps Lisiacensis.	.xli. Radulf de Mortemer.
.vii. Abbatia Glastingberiensis.	.xlii. Robertus filius Giroldi.
.viii. Abbatia Malmesberiensis.	.xliii. Obertus filius Rolf.
.ix. Abbatia Westmonasterii.	.xliiii. Rogerius de Curcelle.
.x. Abbatia Wintoniensis.	.xlv. Rogerius de Berchelai.
.xi. Abbatia Greneburnensis.	.xlvi. Bernard Panceuolt.
.xii. Abbatia Scesfebiensis.	.xlvii. Berenger Gisard.
.xiii. Abbatia Wiltuniensis.	.xlviii. Osbernus Gisard.
.xiiii. Abbatia Wintoniensis.	.xlix. Rogo filius Ponz.
.xv. Abbatia Romesiensis.	.l. Hugo Lasne.
.xvi. Abbatia Ambresberiensis.	.li. Hugo filius Baldrici.
.xvii. Ecclesia Beccensis.	.lii. Hunfrid camerarius.
.xviii. Radulfus presbiter de Wiltune.	.liii. Gunfrid Maldurch.
.xix. Canonici Lisiacensis.	.liiii. Aluredus de Ispania.
.xx. Comes Mortoniensis.	.lv. Wlfus uicecomes.
.xxi. Comes Rogerius.	.lvi. Igellus medicus.
.xxii. Comes Hugo.	.lvii. Osbernus presbiter.
.xxiii. Comes Albericus.	.lviii. Ricard Puingant.
.xxiiii. Eduuard de Sarisberie.	.lix. Odret Marescal.
.xxv. Ernulf de Hesding.	.lx. Robertus Flauus.
.xxvi. Aluredus de Merleberch.	.lxi. Ricardus Sturmis.
.xxvii. Unfridus de Insula.	.lxii. Arnald Canud.
.xxviii. Milo Crispin.	.lxiii. Aiulfus de Moyerania.
.xxix. Isdebertus de Breteuile.	.lxiiii. Gozelin Riuere.
.xxx. Durand de Glouuecestre.	.lxv. Godescal.
.xxxi. Edricus Gisard.	.lxvi. Herman 7 alii seruientes regis.
.xxxii. Wills de Ow.	.lxvii. Odo 7 alii taini regis.
.xxxiii. Wills de Braiose.	.lxviii. Herueus 7 alii ministri regis.
.xxxiiii. Wills de Molin.	
.xxxv. Wills de Faleise.	

Rex habet de Burgo Wilton. 7 e. l. lib. 7 do herueus recepit q[ua]n[do] custodiam reddit. xx.ii. libras.

De Wiltescire h[abe]t rex. xx. lib. p[er] de ap[pendi]tio. 7 xx. solid. p[er] sumario. p[er] seno. c. solid. 7 v. oras.

De dim3 mo[n]ino ap[ud] Sarisberie. h[abe]t rex xx. solid ad pensum.

De t[er]tio denario Sarisberie. h[abe]t rex. vi. lib. De t[er]tio denario Meale berst. xl. lib. De t[er]tio denario euchelase. l. lib. De t[er]tio denario BABE. xl. lib. De t[er]tio denario Malmesberie. xx. lib.

De cremio. lx. lib. ad pondul. h[a]e reddeb[a]t Eduuard9.

Nunc reddeb3 ipsu[m] burgu[m] Malmesberie. 7 redd. uiii. lib. p[er] mel...

TERRA REGIS side:

R[ex] TERRA REGIS.

Rex tenet CALNE. Rex .E. tenuit. Ide[m] n[on] gelda[ui]t. n[ec] scio q[uo]t hidae sint ibi. T[er]ra e[st]. xx.xx. car.

In d[omi]nio sunt .vii. car. 7 vii. seru[i]. Ibi .xxx.vii. uilli 7 xx. bordarii 7 x. cotbr3 cu[m] xxi. car. Ibi sunt .v. burgenses. 7 vii. molini reddentes .iiii. lib. 7 xii. sol. 7 vi. den. 7 lb. 7 xi. pratae. 7 pastura ii. leu[uae] lg. 7 una leu[uae] lat. H[ae]c uilla redd3 firma[m] uni9 noctis cu[m] omib3.

Huic o[mn]i ecclesiam ten[et] Nigell de rege. cu[m] .ii. h[i]d[is] q[uae] p[er]tinent. T[er]ra e[st] .v. car. In d[omi]nio e[st] una 7 iii. seru[i]. Ib[i] vi. uilli 7 ii. bordarii cu[m] ii. car. Ibi .ii. molini de .xx.ii. sol. 7 xxv. burgenses reddu[n]t .xx. sol. Silua in lo[n]g[itudine] lg. 7 una q[uod]q[ue] .xxiii. 7 xii. ac[rae] pastura .iii. q[ua]re[n]t lg .ii. q[ua]rent lat. Tot[um] ual[et] vii. lib.

Aluered de hispania ten. v. hid. o[mn]es q[uas] Nigell esti[m]ab[a]t [per]tin[ere]. h[oc] t[er]ra testimonio scire [per]tinuit ad eccle[sia]m T.R.E.

Rex ten[et] BEDUINE. Rex .E. tenuit. Nu[n]q[uam] geldau[it]. nes h[i]datae fu[erunt]. T[er]ra e[st] q[uo]d .xx. car. una m[isericordia]... In d[omi]nio sunt .xii. car. 7 xii. seru[i]. Ibi q[ui]n[que] .xx. uilli 7 lx. cotezt 7 uiii. salt colibrat. Ibi .viii. molini redd. c. sol. Duae siluae h[abe]nt ii. leu[uae] lg. 7 una leu[uae] lat. Ibi .cc. ac[rae] p[ra]tae. 7 xx. q[ua]r[en]t ex. q[ua]r[en]t. 7 p[er]tin[et] pastura lg. 7 xi. q[uo]dq[ue] lat. Ibi ue de p[ra]n[do] xx. burgenses.

Et cu[m] h[oc] redd3 firma[m] uni9 noctis cu[m] omib3. 7 c[on]suetudin[ibus].

In h[oc] o[mn]i fuer[un]t T.R.E. Lucus habens dim3 leu[uae] lg. 7 q[ua]r[en]t lat. 7 q[ua]re[n]t in d[omi]nio regis. Modo tenet eu[m] henric de ferreris.

Rex ten[et] AMBLESBERIE. Rex .E. tenuit. Nu[n]q[uam] gelda[ui]t. nec hidata fu[it]. T[er]ra e[st] .xl. car. In d[omi]nio sunt .xvi. car. 7 xl. seru[i]. 7 u. colibrat. Ibi q[ui]n[que] .xx. 7 uilli 7 vi. bord[arii] h[abe]nt .xxxvii. car. Ibi .vii. molini redd. iii. lib. 7 x. sol. 7 xx. ac[rae] p[ra]ti. pastura .iii. leu[uae] lg. 7 ii. leu[uae] lat. Silua vi. leu[uae] lg. 7 una leu[uae] lat.

Hoc o[mn]i cu[m] app[endi]ciis suis redd3 firma[m] uni9 noctis.

In h[oc] o[mn]i numerar[un]t t[er]ra m[isericor]... tainos. q[uo]s ipse rex ded[it]. Will[elmo] cu[m] in dobleshie p[er] mutatione bouerans. De hui9 t[er]ra .ii. hid ded[it] rex .E. in sua infirmitate abbatiae Wiltuniensi. q[uae] nu[n]q[uam] antea habuerat. postea u[t] eas tenuit. Et Will[elm] c[omes] de u[ico]... Suindone 7 cheuret q[uae] e[rant] tainlande. p[er]tin[et] de insula de Wich. q[uae] p[er]tinet ad firma[m] de Imbleshore.

Rex ten[et] COTEMARESSE. Rex .E. tenuit. Non geldau[it] nec hidata fu[it]. T[er]ra e[st] .xi. car. In d[omi]nio fu[erunt] vi. car. 7 xiii. seru[i]. 7 xii. porcarii. Ibi xx. uilli 7 viii. cotez3 7 xiii. colibrat. cu[m] xxx. vi. car. Ibi vii. molini de iiii. lib. 7 q[uo]d[que] xx. ac[rae] de t[er]ra. pastura .i. leu[uae] lg. 7 dim3 leu[uae] lat. Silua .ii. leu[uae] lg. 7 ii. leu[uae] lat. 7 dim3 leu[uae] lat.

Hoc o[mn]i redd3 firma[m] uni9 noctis cu[m] omib3. c[on]suetudin[ibus] suis.

Rex ten[et] CHEPEHA[M]. Rex .E. tenuit. Non geldau[it]. nec hidata fu[it]. T[er]ra e[st] .c. car. In d[omi]nio sunt .xvi. car. 7 xviii. seru[i]. Ibi xl. vii. uilli 7 xi. 7 v. bord[arii] 7 xx. col. 7 xviii. porcarii. Int[er] om[ne]s h[abe]nt. lx. vi. car. Ibi xvi. molini de vi. lib. 7 q[uo]dq[ue] x. ac[rae] de p[ra]ti. Silua. iii. leu[uae] lg. 7 ii. leu[uae] lat. pastura lat. 7 lat.

Hoc o[mn]i cu[m] app[endi]ciis suis redd3 firma[m] uni9 noctis cu[m] omib3. 7 c[on]suetudin[ibus]. ual. c. xl. lib. ad numeru[m].

Huic o[mn]i ecclesiam cu[m] ii. hid[is] ten[et] Osb[er]n9 eps ex T.R.E. Una obolum h[a]e u[oca]nt landre. alt[er]a p[ra]n[do] eccle. Tot[um] ual. i.i. solid.

Huic e[st] p[ra]n[do] una t[er]ra qua[m] rex .E. deder[a]t Uluiet uenatori suo. 7 q[uae] e[st] de d[omi]nio suo. h[oc] in firma regis e[st] m[odo]. p[er] hida[m] habebant. T[er]ra e[st] .ii. car. 7 ipsi ibi fu[erunt]. 7 ii. seru[i]. 7 ii. uilli 7 iiii. cotez3 cu[m] i. car. 7 pastura. una q[ua]r[en]t lat. Val. iii. lib.

In firma hui9 o[mn]i e[st] dim3 hid[a] t[er]rae q[uae] fu[it] t[er]ra Uluiet. Edricus tenuit T.R.E.

Bottom continuation:

...radeb3 p[ro]dden3 ipsu[m] burgu[m] T.R.E. 7 in hac firma iacere placita hundred de Cicemone Burelsburg 7 rex p[er]tin3. De moneta p[er]... ipsi burg. e. solid.

...cod burgo habuit herald3 cu[m]... e7 in 7 una m3. masure. 7 vi. aliae uastae. 7 un[um] molin redd. x. solid. hoc t[otu]m reddeb3 .e. sol. T.R.E.

...so p[er]cidit in expeditio[ne] t[er]ra t mari: habet de hoc burgo aut... sol. ad pascendos suos burecar. Aut unu[m] homine[m] ducet secu[m] p[ro] honore .v. hidaru[m].

held and by whom, in 1086, but who held them and what they were worth in the reign of Edward the Confessor. Two successive circuits were made so as to prevent collusion or fraud. Each county record was then arranged by hundreds setting out the various manors which they contained and the properties of all landholders from the King himself and his archbishops down to the villagers and cottagers.

The detailed information that was collected upon the circuits was then processed and the full returns abbreviated. The Norman clerks were less concerned with the counties and hundreds as such than with the honours, baronies or fiefs held directly of the Crown and the estates (or demense) belonging to the King. Thus everything was tidied up according to a recognisable pattern. The abstract or summary of the information which was compiled at Winchester finally constituted a document of four hundred folios and that was, as it was years later pejoratively called, the veritable Great Domesday Book. Some other Domesday records exist (for example, the so-called Little Domesday which was the original return of the East Anglian circuit) and they have revealed to experts precisely how the information was originally collected and in what form. The extraordinary fact about the huge survey was not so much that it was planned as that it was finished. As Professor Galbraith observed, 'the autocratic authority and genius for government of William I pushed to completion a task that proved beyond the strength of later kings'. In consequence of the Domesday survey, William was able scientifically to impose heavy taxation upon his subjects in England during the last year of his reign.

While the Domesday survey was being undertaken, King William himself remained in the south of England; he held Court at Winchester during Easter; on Whit Sunday he was at Westminster; and 1 August he came to Salisbury. Here, writes the Peterborough Chronicler: 'he was met by his council and all the landholders who were of any account throughout England, no matter whose vassals they might be. All did him homage and became his men and swore him oaths of allegiance that they would be faithful to him against all other men.' The significance of the Oath of Salisbury should not be exaggerated or underestimated. There is no reason to imagine that all the

OPPOSITE Domesday Book: a page from the survey of Wiltshire. The book contained a detailed survey of the wealth of the whole of England in 1086; according to the *Anglo-Saxon Chronicle*, the survey was so thorough 'there was not a single hide nor one virgate not even – it is shameful to record it but it did not seem shameful for him to do it – one ox or one cow or pig which escaped notice. . . .'

151

landholders in the kingdom actually assembled upon Salisbury plain to do fealty to their King. It is even doubtful if all the enfeoffed knights came there. What apparently happened was that not only were all the King's tenants-in-chief invited to be present upon this occasion but also their chief military tenants who 'sometimes called themselves "peers" of the honour', and reckoned themselves the social equals of their overlords. Thus it was a grand and splendid gathering and it was also unprecedented in that William required and obtained an oath of fealty both from his 170 tenants-in-chief and also from other important landholders, regardless of their particular status.

It is indeed reasonable to assume that the collecting of information about the wealth of the kingdom (and consequential heavy taxation) were linked together with the Salisbury gathering. Although already by August 1086 the danger of invasion had receded, the King was beset with problems abroad. King Philip I of France was preparing to attack or at least pillage Normandy; William's eldest son Robert was in arms against his father as the ally of the French King; William's half-brother Odo, though safely in prison at Rouen, might easily become the focus of another revolt. In fact, while William had been taking measures to protect his kingdom, his enemies overseas had used the opportunity to stir up trouble for him in and around his duchy. That was why in 1086 William was anxious to be sure that his nobles in England were loyal and that he had available the maximum resources to pay the cost of renewed war. The nobility assembled at Salisbury were not in a position to resist his demands. They recognised that he and they were interdependent; after all, they were all in a conquered country in which they had enriched themselves beyond the dreams of avarice and where, though there might no longer have been seething discontent among the English, whom they had subdued and ousted, sullen resentment certainly remained.

To sum up what still continues to be a highly controversial question (experts on the subject no longer abuse each other as they did in the Victorian age, but they snipe at each other from entrenched positions taken up in academic journals): William did carry out what may fairly be described as revolutionary constitutional changes in England. He imposed a foreign and feudal superstructure upon it. He systematised feudal relationships. That did not mean that he either deliberately or absent-mindedly created states within a state – that is to say the 'honours' with their great lords exercising power, accumulating riches, enlisting armed followers and owning their own castles, household officers, spheres of jurisdiction and a dependent priesthood. Such a systematisation would never have been simple, if steps in that direction by the 'commendation' of thegns to the greater magnates of the realm, proffering services in return for the protection and security of their landed possession, had not already been taking place in Anglo-Saxon England. In the same way it can be argued that the revolutions in seventeenth-century England or eighteenth-century France could never have occurred unless political demands by a rising gentry and professional class at the expense of the old aristocracy had been formulated earlier. Historical events rarely advance (as evolutionary movements have sometimes been supposed to do by scientists) in sudden and inexplicable leaps and bounds. But King William, whether consciously or not, by bringing over his nobility from Normandy to replace the aristocracy that was governing England, had introduced (one must again emphasise) a largely new political, social and economic situation. He may have insisted when he first arrived that he intended to abide by the good old Anglo-Saxon laws and customs and he did do so for three years. Yet in fact he had by his mere conquest made that impossible as a long-term solution. His Frenchmen could not simply step into the shoes of their predecessors; for they did not fit.

ABOVE Silver penny bearing the head of William I. The design is attributed to Theodoric and is dated *c.* 1068.

OPPOSITE An Anglo-Saxon sword.

Will's
nothus

rex wil
lelmi noth'

Lanfranc
nacis

tino
glie
oim
utte
raen
fili
pha
ita
oca
oim
lat
pa
esse
tiox
tob
catu
tue
eus
nari
oso
ina
one

stum
genere lo
crido mense
monachox
tissimum.
decore luc
tum desion
assuptionu
archiepin
marienfis
sa Johann
duca conf
marte
ebrati
que
nena
ibiq
andro

uittmusrubus
thox & itti no
thi scds. tate
sibi pre regnu
anglie duca in
firmitate qm mortuis

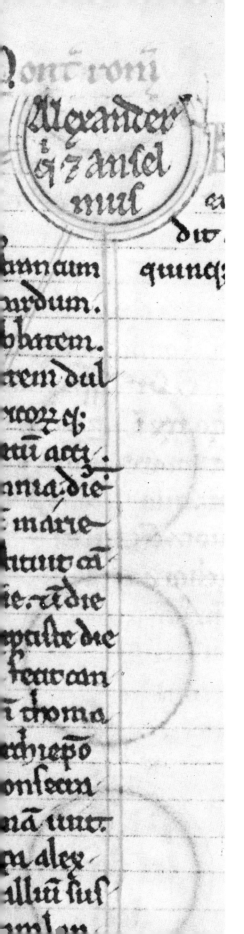

6
The Character of William
1028-87

ALTHOUGH WILLIAM was not the first of the dukes of Normandy to be illegitimate, the opprobrious title of bastard stuck to him all his life and clearly helped to mould his character when he was young. Duke Robert had not in any case been able to marry William's mother, because he was already betrothed, and the arrangement that he made for Arlette to wed one of his *vicomtes* revealed William's illegitimacy plainly enough. It is reasonable to assume that this unimportant black mark merely spurred on William's ambition, that he wanted to compensate himself for it by proving his own outstanding ability. His father's early death provided him with a magnificent opportunity to distinguish himself. He was befriended and knighted by the French King when he was fifteen and by the time he was twenty he was fairly firmly established on his throne.

It was suggested that William's dislike of married clergy (which Queen Elizabeth I was to share many years later) may have been owing to an almost puritanical distaste for what is called sexual immorality. He 'thought it unworthy', wrote William of Poitiers, 'to look with a favourable eye on any cleric who dishonoured himself by irregular behaviour'. After his marriage in 1051, William is believed to have been entirely faithful to his wife; the notion that he was homosexual is doubtful, though he may well have been extremely devoted to his mother who brought him up. He had four sons and several daughters by his wife, Matilda; and although he certainly did not marry her for love, he obviously came to trust her implicitly and allowed her to share all his glories.

The qualities for which William has been given credit include statesmanship, patience, energy, devoutness and temperance. He 'was a man of great wisdom and power,' observed the Peterborough Chronicler, no lover of Normans, 'and surpassed in honour and in strength all those who had gone before him'. William of Jumièges wrote that he was magnanimous, unshaken by toil or danger and patient amid all changes of fortune. About his energy no doubt can exist; he moved swiftly to confront or outmanoeuvre all his enemies; and he took an extraordinary interest in every aspect of government. As to his religious dedication, there is quite a volume of testimony. He and his wife are said to have been most regular in attending their devotions and showed generosity to monasteries. William of

Poitiers observed that: 'Divided between the cares of war and domestic affairs – what are called the worries of the century – this excellent prince directed his highest aspirations towards divine things.' He added that the King followed in the footsteps of his father and granted the prayers only of those clergy and monks who, he thought, were an honour to their profession.

Ordericus Vitalis gives a convincing picture of William's humility and trust in the Almighty on his death-bed and makes him say:

> I have never injured the Church of God, which is our mother, but have always paid her, as circumstances demanded, due honour. I never sold ecclesiastical dignities. I prohibited simony, which I always detested. In the election of prelates my choice was directed by meritorious conduct and wise doctrine, and as far as it has been in my power the government of the Church has been committed to the most worthy.

Like most politicians, he felt that he had a credit balance in his moral account on which he could draw.

With regard to William's temperance, an unknown monk of St Stephen's, Caen, in a description of the King's character which was inserted into the chronicle of William of Jumièges, wrote that he was abstemious in eating and drinking and abhorred drunkenness in himself or others. After his meals, it was noted, he rarely drank more than thrice. The trouble is that this particular sketch of King William, one of the few that have survived, has been shown to have been lifted more or less word for word from the last chapters of an earlier life of the Emperor Charlemagne. Just as a seventeenth-century artist once substituted the face of Cromwell for that of King Charles I in a drawing of him upon horseback, the virtues of Charlemagne were transferred almost bodily to King William. There is no reason (except his corpulence) to suppose that he was temperate, although temperance and energy do not necessarily go together, as witness the eighteenth-century phenomenon Peter the Great of Russia.

So much for William's virtues. On the debit side, it has been said that he was basically an illiterate and uncultured soldier, that he was a brutal oppressor, capable of harshness and cruelty, and that he was extremely greedy. Here understandably the chief witnesses are English writers who urge that he was

naq; corrept' egmonia corpont. millesimo centresimo q̃uo
anno. ab incarnatione dñi uiã petens unīisi gentis humani
gaudentib; anglis diuine uocationis iussu in fine occubuit·

ōn eni indigni estimo crede ipenne officio signare q̃ eũo
celestis intin modatox cul' y sepulcroz locu intrena uenerat
in hui uie medio labore adphempnis q̃te consecratu eu assume
placuerit. He beata anima plurimo iã optimox opũ
splendore candidata pb mundanis actib; implicita mactas
colliget. Sepulti' est etiã inbasilica sc̃e marie. a suis mi ̃
memorips' ciuitatis regñare dñr in patne dextere maiestatis
cũ coequalitate spc̃ sc̃i p omnia sc̃a sc̃loz. ꝯ ⁊ ꞇ ꞇ ꝋ ;

eccensius seruatus Rotbto magni
ducis actib; ex multoz sollertia tridi
gine intimatis auribs; competens
iudetur ut adwillmũ ex filium
uertatur articul' subscribendo
futuris: quo sudore laboris minimoz
laqueos euaserit suisq; eox ferina
colla uesdigiu uirtut' substrauerit·
Plerisq; ō eni scripture reperiũ.

hij igitur nequicia patris uniqui domu̅ filii subuer̅ ⁊
conuerso uero merito b̅oni soleat dñs roborari· Quã deniq;
gc̃ Rodbto duci seræ abeo·   selarib; pompis stabiliui·
dum eum parua numeraueri·   q̃te eni filius q̃ filiũ
uuillinũ pfligauit·   numero trono pbinodũ
                                    piacuit regali· Vscriptam
                                    cuib; uictoriarũ indicauit·

unnecessarily savage in his military campaigns and unmerciful to the poor. Certainly the devastation of the Midlands and the north in 1069 and 1070, though possibly a requirement of warfare, hit the ordinary peasant more than anyone. But if he was harsh and cruel at times, he was never (as Sir Frank Stenton pointed out) blindly tyrannical. Even the Peterborough Chronicler modified his otherwise unattractive portrait of the King by admitting that he kept excellent order:

> ... so that a man of any substance could travel unmolested throughout the country with his bosom full of gold. No man dared to slay another, no matter what evil the other might have done him. If a man lay with a woman against her will, he was forthwith condemned to forfeit those members with which he had disported himself.

The accusation that William was avaricious – an accusation that has generally been levelled against conquerors – is also naturally derived chiefly from English chroniclers, but it has been accepted even by his admirers among modern historians. The English were, as has been seen, heavily taxed in order to pay for his mercenaries and foreign wars. To the Peterborough Chronicler, who was by no means unfair to him, William was 'very stark' and the scribe broke out into a famous doggerel verse about him:

> He was sunk in greed
> And utterly given up to avarice.
> He set apart a vast deer preserve and
> Imposed laws concerning it.
> Whoever slew a hart or hind
> Was to be blinded.
> He forbade the killing of boars
> Even as the killing of harts.
> For he loved the stags as dearly
> As though he had been their father.

He also laid it down, according to this poet, that hares should 'go unmolested'; although rich and poor alike complained that 'he was too relentless to care even if all might hate him'.

The vast 'deer preserve' which he created was the New Forest in Hampshire, as it is still known today. Ordericus Vitalis wrote that after William became King, 'being a great lover of forests, he laid waste more than sixty parishes ... and

OPPOSITE A page from the chronicle of William of Jumièges, a monk of that house who wrote a sober account of the life of William up to 1071. (Ms Bodley 517, f. 26v.)

substituted beasts of the chase for human beings that he might satisfy his ardour for hunting'. The extent of the damage done to the livelihoods of ordinary Englishmen by William's adding about one third to this forest area within easy reach of Winchester can be exaggerated. It has been pointed out that Anglo-Saxon kings were equally fond of hunting and owned their private chases, that heath and scrubland were of little value to agriculture, and that only villages on the outskirts of the New Forest were destroyed. Still, special forest laws of growing severity were introduced from Normandy and the size of the royal forests was increased as compared with what it was in Saxon times. It was a grievance which gnawed at all classes, and the peak of protest against the forest laws was to be reached at the time of Magna Carta. The New Forest became a symbol of William's greed; and in the twelfth century chroniclers were to point out that the deaths in the New Forest of several of William's descendants, including that of his second son Richard, his third son William (Rufus) and his grandson Richard constituted divine punishment for the crime against his subjects.

William was very much the personal ruler of the kingdom and therefore had to bear the full responsibility for his decisions. His Court or *curia* was merely asked for advice which might or might not be taken. The King had the invaluable knack of being able to find good and reliable servants and clearly took notice of what men like Archbishop Lanfranc said to him. He was a consummate politician; but whether, in spite of his victories in Normandy and at Hastings, he was more than a second-rate soldier may be doubted. He had, however, the gift of leadership. Even when he campaigned in the depths of winter under severe conditions of frost and snow, he encouraged his troops by his enterprise, bravery and cheerfulness. He often led the way on foot and was always ready himself to help his men out of their particular difficulties. Capable of facing every deprivation, even living on the flesh of horses which had perished in bogland, he despised the cowards who deserted him and refused to conciliate them with offers of future rewards. All he would promise (according to Ordericus Vitalis) was ultimate rest to those of his followers who overcame the hardships of a winter campaign 'declaring that there was no

OPPOSITE Trees in the New Forest. William created the New Forest in Hampshire so that he could indulge his passion for hunting. Some villages were depopulated for this purpose and severe penalties imposed upon those who stole the royal game.

OPPOSITE William the
Conqueror surrounded by
knights in armour, from
a fourteenth-century
manuscript. Below him
is shown his line
of descendants.

road to honour except by hard exertions'. But though he was a brave and at times a swift leader, he contributed nothing new to the evolution of strategy or tactics.

As a diplomatist, William was astute, knowing when to compromise (as he did with King Swein) and when to fight. But where he excelled was as a propagandist: the story which he spread and was believed by the Pope, by contemporary rulers and by some modern historians that he was the accepted and lawful heir to the English throne, the story which was epitomised in the narrative of William of Poitiers, though in fact it can be shown to be riddled with inaccuracies and improbabilities, and has been preserved for posterity in the Bayeux Tapestry, was a masterpiece of propaganda, even by modern standards, an example of the way in which if a story is told often enough it is assumed to be true. William lived in a world in which deception was a fact of life. Another piece of clever propaganda for which he was responsible is that he actually preserved and upheld the institutions and ancient laws of the Anglo-Saxons. Certainly he said that it was his intention to do so. Yet one has only to remember the supersession of the hundred courts by the church courts in deciding spiritual questions, or the introduction of the strict forest laws, or the transformation of the sheriffs, to realise that though some traditional English practices might have been adapted to Norman needs, to a limited extent and perhaps unconsciously, William was a revolutionary.

What did William look like? Not much is known for certain because his portraits are either stylised (as in the Bayeux Tapestry) or speculative and imaginative. One or two things, however, seem to be firmly established. He was five feet ten inches in height, was 'robust' or 'burly' and grew heavier in weight during his later life. He also had a harsh or rough voice. His Queen, whose bones still lie buried in the church of Holy Trinity, Caen, is known (because these bones were disinterred some twelve years ago) to have been only four feet tall. They must indeed have been an odd-looking couple: William, nearly six feet tall and of a considerable bulk with his four-foot wife, presumably slimmer, trotting along beside him.

They had several children. The eldest son, Robert Curthose, was to follow in the footsteps of his grandfather by going to the

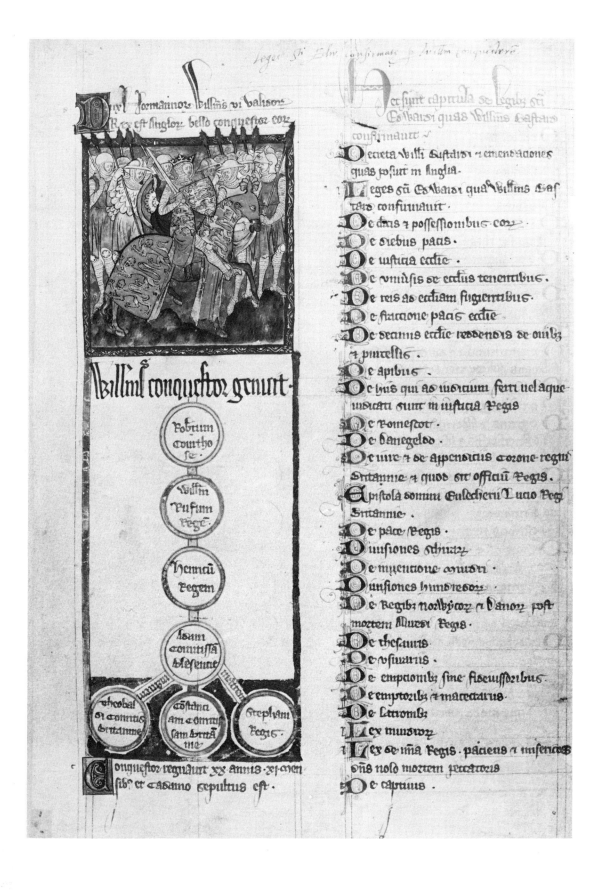

The tomb of Robert Curthose, Duke of Normandy, in Gloucester Cathedral. Although he had constantly rebelled against his father, William forgave him on his death-bed and bequeathed to him the duchy of Normandy. The kingdom of England, however, went to William's third son, William Rufus, his second son having died c. 1075.

Silver denim of Robert,
Duke of Normandy.

Middle East upon the First Crusade. Nevertheless the monkish chroniclers did not admire his treatment of the Church when he succeeded his father as Duke of Normandy; he allowed himself to be bullied or outmanœuvred by his younger brothers and died a royal prisoner. Robert was his mother's darling and she even tried to help him out of her own resources to maintain a military force. William angrily said 'a faithless woman is her husband's bane'. But the Queen defended herself and William forgave her for her partiality towards their eldest son.

Their second son, Richard, was accidentally killed in the New Forest when young. Their third son, William 'Rufus', that is 'red-faced', was corpulent like his father and inherited at least some of his ability; by repute he was not a Christian, and he was a homosexual. The fourth son, Henry 'Beauclerk' had a quite unjustified reputation for learning, because he was as illiterate and uneducated as his father. Henry was the ablest of the four sons. He is said to have been fond of animals because he kept a zoo at Woodstock, but that did not prevent his killing stags.

William's eldest daughter was Agatha: she predeceased her father, dying on her way to Spain where she was going to marry the King of Castile. His second daughter, Adeliza, became a nun as did also his third daughter, Cecily, who was appointed Abbess of Holy Trinity, Caen, which her mother had founded. Another daughter, Adela, married the Count of Blois in 1080 and by him became the mother of Stephen, the last of the Norman kings of England. Finally, Constance, who may or may not have been William's youngest daughter, was married towards the end of her father's life to Count Alan IV of Brittany, thus cementing an old family alliance. William attended the wedding at Bayeux in 1086. By then his wife, Queen Matilda, was already dead: she disappeared from life in November 1083 and also disappeared from history. Professor Barlow tells us that 'she remains a completely colourless figure'; but she did not escape the usual pious platitudes. Her epitaph at Caen read in part:

> . . . 'twas here her holiest work was seen,
> This shrine, this house where cloistered sisters dwell,
> And with their notes of praise the anthem swell,
> Endowed and beautified her earnest care.
> Nor others failed her liberal aims to share;
> The sick, the indigent gained from her store,
> She laid up wealth by giving to the poor.

William spent most of his last months in Normandy, though his movements are not completely known. He feared that the French King, Philip I, was intending to undermine the security of the duchy by an attack from the east. There had always been unrest on the frontier known as the Vexin: in fact two Vexins confusingly existed. The Norman Vexin was an integral part of Normandy lying between the rivers Andelle and Epte, while the county of Vexin lay between the Epte and the Oise. The Count of Vexin held his territory as a vassal of the French King, but when in 1077 a Count named Simon had elected to opt for

William Rufus, who became King of England on the death of his father, William I. In August 1100, William II was mysteriously killed by an arrow while hunting in the New Forest. Many writers in the twelfth century felt that this was divine vengeance for the savage methods his father had used when instituting the New Forest as his hunting preserve.

169

chastity and to enter a monastery on or immediately after his wedding night, King Philip I had personally occupied the county, which then became known as the French, as distinct from the Norman, Vexin. William, whose attentions at the time were distracted elsewhere, reluctantly acquiesced in this act of French expansion. Philip I in fact had good reasons for wishing to govern the area, since it lay within thirty miles of his capital, Paris.

Disturbances constantly prevailed on this Norman-French frontier. When, in the summer of 1087, the garrison at Mantes, capital of the French Vexin, crossed the frontier to pillage, William planned a counter-offensive with the object of annexing the French Vexin. It was partly in order to pay for this campaign that he had levied such heavy taxes upon England following the Domesday survey.

William led an army across the River Epte, laid waste much of the French Vexin, burning the corn and rooting up the vines, and surprised the garrison of Mantes by the speed of his advance. The town was set on fire by the retreating French defenders and was given over to the sack by the Normans. As William was riding among the burning ruins, he was suddenly injured or taken severely ill – it is not clear which. Possibly his frightened horse leapt and threw its rider against the pommel of his saddle or else, in the words of Ordericus Vitalis, being 'very corpulent', the King 'fell sick from the excessive heat and his great fatigues'. At any rate he was incapacitated and after six weeks was taken back to his capital of Rouen. But he found the noise of the city insupportable and ordered that he should be carried to the priory of St Gervais which stood on a hill to the west of Rouen. Here he summoned his sons William and Henry to his death-bed (his eldest son Robert was at the Court of his enemy, the French King). William Bonne-Ame, the Archbishop of Rouen (who had succeeded John of Avranches on his death in 1079) also watched over his Duke, while a bishop and an abbot skilful in medicine 'devoted themselves to their master's welfare, both spiritual and temporal'.

Ordericus Vitalis has left us an edifying and moving picture of William the Conqueror's last days. He puts words into the mouth of the dying King which have been accepted as plausible, though imaginative, by later biographers. 'My friends, I

170

Martino sedé dedit hic sansonis in ede ·   Ecclia sci martani
Nciola sedis sed voca rudida sede
Adda ponenda sui qd lebec ad faciendu

PHILIP REX

Ecclia sci sansonis subiecta bexto martino

richer   Gaufrid· Gyrdo Gaufrer· hugor rogor· hu
senon
arch
epe

raimald· wellelm· hugo   hugo fr· baldwin· willelm drogo arch wido demer
comes   comes   comes regis comes   gluser   pariensis erbriaco

William Rufus (left) and
Henry I (right). Henry I,
the youngest son of
William the Conqueror.
succeeded his brother on
the throne in 1100.
Henry I was succeeded by
by his nephew Stephen,
the last of the Norman
kings of England.

172

pci ipitt' le rois frcs
nale vn mer henri

tremble,' he is made to say, 'when I reflect on the grievous sins which burden my conscience, and now, about to be summoned before the awful tribunal of God, I know not what I ought to do. I was bred to arms from my childhood, and am stained with the rivers of blood that I have shed.' It is curious to reflect that another, later king, who was a practising Christian and was to die in France over six centuries and a quarter later – Louis XIV – was also to confess: 'I was too fond of war.' William explained it was not altogether his fault. He had been thrust into the dukedom of Normandy at the age of seven and since then he had always been a soldier. His subjects, including his own relatives, had often rebelled against him, for the Normans, when they were not occupied in fighting their enemies abroad, were accustomed to 'rend in pieces and ruin each other'.

William went on to describe what he had suffered at the hands of the kings of France who had invaded or pillaged his duchy and how he had also been perfidiously attacked at times by his neighbours, the counts of Anjou, Brittany and Flanders. In this speech he is not given a great deal to say about England, except to regret his oppressions and to take pride in his victories over the many peoples, from Scots to Danes, who had vainly attempted to deprive him of his rightful crown. But he is attributed with adding 'much as human ambition is disposed to triumph in such successes, I am prey to cruel fears and anxieties when I reflect with what barbarities they were accompanied'.

The dying King tried to salve his conscience by directing that his treasure in Rouen should be given to the churches and to the poor, and he reiterated that he had never harmed or exploited the Church of God. On the contrary, he believed that the monasteries and nunneries that he had built in Normandy were fortresses in which men and women were taught 'to combat the demons and sins of the flesh'. He begged his two sons to follow in that respect his own example and to learn from pious philosophers how to distinguish good from evil.

Although his eldest son had fought against him and had now deserted him, William confirmed Robert's succession as Duke of Normandy, for a grant, once solemnly given, could not be annulled. But he appointed his third son, William, to replace him as King of England and, according to Ordericus, gave him a letter which he was to take immediately to Archbishop

174

William Conquestor Bastard
Kyng Normandie

Anno gͩo mͦllͦ lxbij ...
kalend, Januꝛ Coronat
Apd westͫ willͫ conqꝫ
ꝑim Anno regni dni xxͦ
Cadomi tumulat. hͦ
pax a iusticie inuiolabꝭ
ꝑuator existit ẜat
Puella Anio omꝫ regni
Anglie ꝑfect supuit.

The nyne William duke of Normandy
As bokis old makith mension.
Be juste titill & bi his chivalri.
Was kyng bi conquest of Brutf Albion.
Put out Harold and toke possession.
And hasse the governaunce of his region.
He governid his lond as is to tell.
Fille on a time that it bi felle.
As the cronikyll welle telle can.
Off this gentil Duke William.
At Westm William y crownid was.
The ffirst day of Cristesmas.

Grete ryng he after did than.
Mase ye kyng of Scottis his legeman.
Also of every hide of ye lond by & by.
In England he toke vf to truly.
He regnid here xxi yere.
Bi jond ye see he lieth there.
In Normandi he deid at hame.
And is y buried in ye Abbei of Cane.
He gafe his eldir son Normandi.
And to ye secund England trewly.
And to ye pirde his godie mevabill.
This was holde ferme and stabille.

Lanfranc so as to make sure of the throne. To his youngest son, Henry, he bequeathed only £5,000 in silver, which was received without enthusiasm, though it was to be quickly collected. Again according to Ordericus, William forecast that Henry would surpass the other two in wealth and power. But here this brilliant historian must have been employing hindsight, as historians do.

It has in fact been argued by a distinguished modern historian, John Le Patourel – himself of Norman descent, or at any rate a Channel Islander – that it cannot have been William's original intention to divide up the 'Anglo-Norman' state, to which Maine had been added, the state that he himself had devoted most of his life to creating. It is true that some early medieval rulers, Charlemagne is an obvious case, had been obliged to partition their territories among their children when they died, but that was not a tradition among the dukes of Normandy. Probably, it is contended, William's first instinct, which was natural enough, was to pass on the inheritance intact to his eldest son. But two difficulties had arisen. The first was that William and Robert had been constantly on bad terms with each other and when his father was waging his last fight, Robert was in the camp of William's chief enemy. The other difficulty was that William could hardly have transferred the entire inheritance to his namesake, who was reputedly his favourite, because Robert Curthose had been solemnly invested with the titles of Duke of Normandy and Count of Maine at an early age, even if he had been refused any real authority.

Yet up to the very end, it seems, William was reluctant to split up his dominions. 'It was only,' writes Professor Le Patourel, 'when the archbishop of Rouen and others who were beside the dying king's bedside intervened on Robert's behalf, and William was evidently too weak to resist, that he accepted a kind of compromise. ...' In fact, as subsequent history relates, both William Rufus and Henry I were able to reunify England and Normandy, though it required further acts of chicanery and conquest. The Battle of Tinchebrai, contested forty years after he was dead by William's two surviving sons, placed the seal on Anglo-Norman union until, nearly a century and a half after the Norman conquest, the duchy was lost by King John.

On Thursday, 9 September 1087, William woke early in the

176

RIGHT A Scandinavian riding to war, from a twelfth-century tapestry. The Scandinavian menace remained present in William's reign, although Harold Hardrada's invasion of 1066 was the last major Viking assault on England.

BELOW An army on the move, from an eleventh-century manuscript from the Benedictine abbey of Monte Cassino in Italy: *Encyclopaedia of Maurus Hrabanus*.

ABOVE St Stephen's, Caen, the
church of the Abbaye-aux-Hommes
founded by William.
RIGHT The plain stone slab in
St Stephen's Church, Caen, which
records what was the burial place
of William the Conqueror. The
slab was erected in the nineteenth
century, earlier monuments
having been destroyed.

†
HIC SEPULTUS EST
INVICTISSIMUS
GUILLELMUS
CONQUESTOR,
NORMANNIÆ DUX,
ET ANGLIÆ REX,
HUJUSCE DOMUS,
CONDITOR,
QUI OBIIT ANNO
M.LXXXVII.

An imaginery scene from a
fourteenth-century manuscript
showing William landing with
his troops and baggage in Gascony.
As far as it is known, William
never went to Gascony.

morning and listened to the sound of the great bell of Rouen Cathedral tolling. He asked the attendants what it meant. 'My Lord,' was the answer, 'the bell is tolling for the Prime [a service at sunrise] in the church of St Mary.' The King himself then spoke in prayer: 'I commend myself to Mary, the Holy Mother of God, my heavenly mistress, that by her blessed intercession, I may be reconciled to her beloved son, Our Lord Jesus Christ.' After that, he died instantly.

The Archbishop of Rouen ordered that the King should be buried in the monastery of St Stephen at Caen, the twin of the nunnery of Holy Trinity in which his wife had been interred. The body was embalmed and taken by hearse to the Seine; then it was carried by boat down the river and thence by land to Caen. Many distinguished mourners were present at the funeral, and a sermon was preached by Bishop Gilbert of Lisieux. Unhappily the big and heavy body was broken as it was being lowered into the sepulchre which the stonemasons had made too short. In the sixteenth century, the tomb was despoiled and the monument erected in William's memory demolished by Calvinists. A new monument was later vandalised by the revolutionaries of 1793. Today, only a plain slab in the abbey church at Caen records that the first Norman king of England had been buried there.

7
Economic and Social Life in the Reign of William 1066-87

NEARLY THE WHOLE POPULATION of England in the reign of William I was engaged in agriculture and most of the peasantry were absorbed in arable farming. 'Ploughland' and 'plough teams' were frequent words in the Domesday survey; every estate had its quota of ploughs, while other ploughs were owned jointly or individually by villagers. It is estimated that seven to eight million acres in the kingdom were under cultivation. But the area of land which could be tilled was limited by vast forests (such as the New Forest) and untamed woodland (like the Weald) and there was also much useless heath and scrub.

The essential need was to grow grain; for that was wanted not only to feed men and animals but to provide barley out of which ale, the principal beverage, was made. No doubt the majority of peasants lived on or below a marginal subsistence level according to whether the climate was beneficent and the soil fertile. Sheep farming was less common than it was to become later and was actually on the decline. Flocks of from eight hundred to two thousand sheep are known to have flourished in parts of the kingdom; but sheep farming was chiefly concentrated in eastern and south-western England. Meadows were comparatively few and cattle were put out to graze on marshlands and fenlands and quite often on arable land, presumably when it lay fallow.

Pigs were more generally kept than sheep; for pigs could be fed in woodland. Pig-keepers might have to pay for the right to use the woodland with a rent in kind which was known as 'pannage'. Not many cows were to be found, milk being obtained from goats or ewes. Honey provided sweetening for food, while salt-pans offered a means of preserving meat during the winter. Inland waters also yielded food; eels were in eager demand as well as salmon and trout. Sea-fishing mainly produced herrings.

Although the Norman scribes who compiled Domesday Book thought in terms of manors, England was a kingdom made up of villages and hamlets. The hamlets (or scattered households numbering two to five) were to be found chiefly in pasture country, while villages were centres of arable farming whence peasants set out with their ploughs, carts or barrowloads of seed to work in fields or on manorial estates. It has been said that so many villages and hamlets existed throughout the land

ABOVE Ploughing with a Saxon ox-plough, an illustration for January from an eleventh-century calendar. Behind the plough, a man follows scattering seeds.

PREVIOUS PAGES Scene from an eleventh-century calendar showing men reaping with scythes.

that they were mostly within easy reach of one another: thus it was 'a world of neighbours'. It is not known how the village communities were organised. Most villages had a church and a priest (who cultivated the glebeland belonging to his church and was the social equal and rarely the superior of his parishioners). Whether beside the church they also enjoyed an alehouse is a guess: surely they must have done. Either a village reeve or a manorial reeve directed agricultural operations. The lands belonging to the villagers were distributed in open fields, and arrangements had to be made about ploughs and the use of the waste.

The peasants were divided into four classes: first 'free men' (*liberi homines*) and 'sokemen'. 'Soke' meant jurisdiction, so sokemen were men who owned their land but were expected to attend the courts of their lords, to help them at busy seasons and to pay them a small monetary tribute. They were principally but not exclusively to be discovered in eastern England which, when it was settled by the Danes, who were warriors turned into agricultural settlers, had a rather different kind of economy and different customs from the rest of the country. During William's reign the numbers of freemen and sokemen declined sharply, particularly in the eastern counties. The Normans looked with suspicion on modest peasant proprietors who could

Scenes from a medieval
book showing the
occupations of the months.

Top row, left to right:
January – a man cooking
and warming his feet
before a fire;
February – ditching, a man
holds an iron spade and
pitcher; March – pruning;
April – planting trees.

Centre row: May – a rich
man hawking; June – cutting
thistles; July – cutting grass
with a scythe; August –
reaping.

Bottom row: September –
threshing with flail;
October – sowing;
November – slaughtering
an ox with an axe;
December – a rich man
feasting.

Martius

Aprilis

Iulius

Augustus

Nouember

December

'go with their land wherever they would'. There is no reason to suppose that these men had any larger holdings than the average villager or *villanus*. This second class of peasant consisted of smallholders, generally with about thirty acres of their own to cultivate, and they constituted two-fifths of the total population. They paid rent to their landlords in three different ways. As a rule they were expected to do unpaid work on the manorial 'demesne' or 'inland', as often as two days a week and three at harvest time; money rents were quite usual, in fact they were commoner than once used to be thought; finally food rents were paid, for example with eggs and chickens.

The third class of peasant were cottagers (*cotarii* and *bordarii*) who led varied lives. As they usually had only one to five acres of their own land to cultivate, they relied on others for a livelihood as shepherds, ploughmen, swineherds or blacksmiths: nevertheless, by way of rent they were required to give a day or more of their time each week or to work at harvest time for nothing. Quite commonly they fulfilled their obligations by working on Mondays and thus were to be known as 'Monday men'. The last class to be found among the English peasantry were slaves (*servi*). Some twenty-five thousand of them existed in 1066. Whether the Normans disapproved of slaves on religious grounds or merely thought they were uneconomic, slavery was gradually disappearing during William's reign. All these classes of peasant had their specific duties and privileges; thus there was little that was arbitrary about their lives except their dependence on the weather. Villagers, on the whole, were not too badly off in those days. But a reduction in their status lay ahead. Before the early Middle Ages ended, the 'villan' was becoming a serf.

The peasants in Norman England did not all have the same kind of landlords. The owners of really big estates – the tenants-in-chief – set out to extract the maximum amounts of money that they could get out of them. Such men have been compared to the beneficiaries of take-over bids in twentieth-century England. Thus they did not usually farm their own demesne or 'inland' directly: they either leased it for a fixed money rent or 'farm', allowing the lessees or farmers to make what profit they could out of the arrangement, or they might

ABOVE Minstrels with cymbals, an early harp and a lute from the *Encyclopaedia of Maurus Hrabanus*, an eleventh-century manuscript from the abbey of Monte Cassino.

BELOW Three lords drinking while, on the right, a horn-player entertains them; from an eleventh-century manuscript.

put the exploitation of the land into the hands of reeves or bailiffs, thus permitting them to earn a valuable commission. This method was followed by the King himself and inevitably aroused grievances since the farmers' intentions were to maximise their profits at all costs. The Peterborough Chronicler wrote:

> The King and the leading men were fond, too fond of avarice: they coveted gold and silver and they did not care how sinfully it was obtained as long as it came to them. The King granted his land on the highest terms and at the highest possible price. If another buyer came and offered more than the first had given, the King would let it go to the man who offered him more. If a third came and offered still more, the King would make it over to the man who offered him most of all. He did not care at all how very wrongfully the reeves got possession of it from wretched men, nor how many illegal acts they did . . . .

Nevertheless, one factor favoured the peasants. In the northeast of England, which had formed part of 'the Danelaw', a tradition of freedom still prevailed, though it was eroded. Wherever the village lands were divided amongst several estates (that is, under the ownership of different manorial lords), as was often the case in northern as well as eastern England, this secured more independence for the villagers.

It is reasonable to assume that the economy in the 'demesne' lands differed considerably from that in the ordinary peasant holdings. The lord, or in fact usually his bailiff or farmer, might often have found it profitable to vary his produce according to the character of the district and the demands of the market. Thus sheep would be grazed to produce wool and meat, horses might be bred and cheese manufactured, even though corngrowing was the essence of the economy. At the same time the *villani* and other classes who were expected to do work in the demesne possibly received perquisites. As R. V. Lennard wrote:

> The villagers of the Conqueror's day, like their successors a few generations later, may well have received an occasional meal in return for their 'boonworks', and herrings from a distance, and perhaps cheese that had been made on some other manor of their lord, may have formed part of their diet when they were thus employed, while the clothing they wore and the implements they used may not improbably have been fashioned in part out of materials which were not strictly local products . . .

190

Norman cooks preparing a feast for William and his nobles; a scene from the Bayeux Tapestry. On the left, two men are boiling meat in big pot suspended over a fire on forked poles. Above is a row of chickens on spits. In the centre, a baker stands by his oven and uses large tongs to take the cooked loaves from the oven and put them on a trencher. On the right, the cooked food is handed to servers to take to the tables.

Still, in general, their standard of living would have been determined by their own exertions which would rarely have lifted them above a minimal subsistence level.

Industry and commerce played a comparatively minor part in the national economy. There had been tin mines in Cornwall since Roman times and lead mines in Derbyshire. Iron works were scattered all over the kingdom, in the Sussex Weald, in the Forest of Dean, in Lincolnshire, Northamptonshire and Yorkshire. Salt works, which were widely distributed, may be described as industrial. It is surprising that the Norman Conquest did not stimulate commerce, for trade had previously been active between England and Normandy, but it does not appear to have done so. Town life, however, received a slight fillip. The building of castles protected local markets; in fact,

William's nobility discovered that they could derive financial advantage by encouraging the establishment of new markets. But most markets were to be found in county towns. On the other hand, Norman ruthlessness, for instance at York, was damaging to urban life. Domesday Book, remarked Mr Lennard – who knew it almost by heart – does not convey the impression of urban economy being vitalised by the Normans. 'The towns were few and tiny,' he wrote, 'industry and commerce were on a small scale. The rich man was a landlord, and land was the source of his riches.' The only considerable cities were London, Norwich and York. William saw that they paid the utmost for their privileges, such as the right to mint coins, but did not grant new ones. Most county boroughs were valuable sources of revenue for the Crown. Perhaps the only notable way in which the King helped trade was to permit Jews to settle in England. A Jewish colony had flourished in Rouen and was now allowed in London. In the long run, Jewish enterprise contributed to the expansion of trade and commerce.

How far were the English people assisted by the strengthening of the law and the reorganisation of the law courts under King William? As has been observed already, after his conquest, the King promised to uphold the existing laws and customs of the land. The actual words which he used were that all should have 'the laws of King Edward in lands and in all things, having added thereto the things which I have appointed for the welfare of the people of the English'. The structure of the county courts and hundred courts remained intact except that the spiritual courts were introduced. The county courts or 'shire moots' were not only law courts but associations for the administration of defence and taxation, while the hundred courts were, besides being jurisdictional centres, unions for the purpose of exacting feudal dues and public and military services. In brief, they were both an integral part of the government of the kingdom. But they were more easily used to enforce duties than to uphold rights. For the difficulty was how to discover what laws and customs there were which had to be maintained since they were incredibly complex and confused. There was, for instance, Wessex law and Mercian law as well as Danelaw. Equally, private jurisdictions had been lavishly granted in Anglo-Saxon

OPPOSITE A map of the world from an eleventh-century manuscript, *The Marvels of the East*. In the lower left-hand corner, England and Scotland can be seen. In the upper part of the map, Mesopotamia and Arabia are identified. Almost in the centre is Mount Olympus, and to the right of this, a fort on a promontary is named Alexandria.

England consisting of 'sac and soc' (though nobody knows precisely what that meant), 'toll and team' – 'toll' being the right to impose a sales tax and 'team' being the right to hold a court to establish ownership of property – and 'infangenetheof', the right to punish a thief caught in the act. Such rights, enforcible by private courts, detracted from the authority of the public law courts and were regarded by the compilers of Domesday Book as property rights along with the possession of cattle or slaves. What William did in order to sort out the confusion was to rely upon the sheriffs to supervise the administration of justice in the county and hundred courts. Whereas previously the sheriffs had usually been secondary landowners, under William they were rich and influential aristocrats, similar to the *vicomtes* of Normandy. These sheriffs often used their offices to feather their own nests and if justice were to be upheld, the royal administration had to keep them under constant surveillance. The second way in which William aimed to strengthen royal justice was by sending members of his own court to conduct important trials in the county courts, though in fact these cases generally dealt with disputes between the well-to-do over property rights.

'It is clear', wrote Sir Frank Stenton, 'that the Norman kings established the jury as a regular part of the machinery of English government.' But during the reign of William the Conqueror this was not the jury of 'twelve good men and true' whose verdicts were to determine criminal cases in later days. The juries employed in the eleventh century were 'juries of inquest' who were required to swear the truth as to facts. For example, during the taking of the Domesday survey, juries, consisting of a village priest, the reeve and six other villagers, were invited to furnish information about the ownership of property. This institution appears to have been brought over from Normandy. On the other hand, it is known that in the 'wapentakes' – equivalent to 'hundreds' in the English Danelaw – twelve leading thegns were required to point out criminals after swearing not to accuse innocent men. But again, these thegns did not give a verdict in criminal cases, which were concluded by primitive means. So, Stenton added, 'it becomes difficult to regard the jury simply as a Norman device transplanted by act of state to England'. Moreover the establishment of the jury

ɪꞇ ny̆ꞅ aꝼɑnꝺoꝺ · ꝼꞅꞇɑh hꞃæꝥeꞃe ꝥæꞃɑ by̆ꞃlɑ
epeꞅ æꞅꞇenꝺe ·

ꝥ ꝼɑꞃɑꝺ mæꞇꞇe ꝥæꞇ héꞅꞇoꝺe beɑꞃꞃe ꞇɑ · ꟷꞌhɪm ꝼ ꝥ unɪɑ
ꞅ̇ɑn up oꝼꝥɑɪm ꝼloꝺꞃ ꞃꞇoꞃon ꝼæꞅꞃe oꞃɑn · ꟷɪꞃpɪꞃe
ꝺe onmoꞃꞁꞅum lɑnꝺe · hɪmꝥuhꞇɑ ꞇɑc ꝥæꞇ · y̆ꞅlɑac ɪu

A king sitting in council and, on the
right, an execution, from an eleventh-
century manuscript. In Norman
England the administration of justice
was enforced through an intricate
system of county courts, hundred
courts, spiritual courts and private
jurisdictions, but the king was
in effect the ultimate source
of justice.

as a regular part of civil judicial procedure in England owed much, it has been pointed out, to the Anglo-Saxon invention of the sealed writs. These 'economically-worded documents' enabled the King's commands to be carried to distant quarters of his realm.

The only novelty that the Normans appear to have introduced into English criminal law was the right in certain cases for judicial decisions to be reached by the prosecutor and the defendant fighting each other: this was called 'trial by battle' and was no more satisfactory than the old English method of finding out whether an accused man was guilty or innocent by throwing him into a river to see if he floated or sank. In fact Englishmen were allowed to choose between trial by ordeal and trial by battle. But Frenchmen were given greater privileges for if they were accused of a crime by Englishmen and did not wish to submit to proof of a crime by judgment or a duel then they were permitted to purge themselves 'by an unbroken oath'.

The Normans continued to create private jurisdictions. These, together with the spiritual courts and the occasional interventions in the shire courts, did not simplify the law of the land but further complicated it. What with the different codes of law and custom, which continued to be respected, some admixture of Norman and Roman law, and the new or additional courts, the Normans did little to improve or consolidate the law and so far as the catching of criminals was concerned it remained basically primitive. One novelty consequent upon the Conquest was a rule that if a person was found dead and could not be proved to be English, he was presumed to be a Norman and the hundred became liable for a murder fine. If justice could not be obtained in the hundred court, the case could, as in Anglo-Saxon times, be referred to the county court, but a central law court was still lacking. William was in no real sense the 'fountain of justice' as some of his successors were to be.

Nevertheless, William and his nobility, with their servants and soldiers, managed to establish and keep peace and order. The tribute by the Anglo-Saxon Chronicler, which has already been quoted, about a man being able to 'travel unmolested throughout the country with his bosom full of gold' is impartial evidence of the degree of security that was imposed. Professor

David Douglas once wrote that 'the restoration of order in English society' was 'incomparably' one of 'the most important results of the Norman conquest'. Yet the last fifteen years or so of the reign of Edward the Confessor were peaceable and prosperous. In the long run the Normans enforced internal peace but it was purchased at a high price. It is arguable that whereas the upper classes were better off under William because they felt more secure, the peasants, who constituted the mass of the population, were not.

Were they in fact worse off? It is easy to stress the continuity of rural life. The regular pattern of the agricultural year from sowing to harvest time, from the sufferings of the winter to the joys of spring, could scarcely be affected by external causes. Again, families that were in fact living on or about the marginal subsistence level were hard to exploit, while conditions were bound to vary from county to county and manor to manor. No doubt some peasants were able to improve their incomes while others could not. What is clear is that whereas slavery was in the process of being abolished in William's reign, the number of freemen, who were chiefly concentrated in the eastern counties in 1066, was, if one may judge by the records in Domesday Book, being substantially reduced. That was a change in status not in wealth. Still, signs have been detected that in parts of the kingdom the numbers of cottagers increased at the expense of villagers with larger holdings, possibly because smallholders were ruined by political and social disorders or by heavy taxation. That would have meant a genuine economic decline. On balance, it is also plain that there was pressure towards a uniform status for peasants from both above and below. The Normans may (as Professor Barlow points out) merely have accelerated a process which had already begun earlier.

Leaving aside the questions of status, did the peasants experience hardships under Norman rule? It has been shown from the Domesday records that in parts of the kingdom, notably in southern and eastern England, rents were rising and even becoming oppressive. Thus the evidence in the *Anglo-Saxon Chronicle* of deliberate exploitation both by the King himself and by the new aristocracy is confirmed. Beyond doubt also, devastation of northern England and part of the Midlands, carried out by King William and his soldiers for military reasons

at the beginning of the reign, was injurious to the rural classes there, creating havoc and famine, while the building of castles generally led to the destruction of property. Even in areas which were not so tragically affected as those that were ravaged in 1069 and 1070 (observes Professor Douglas) 'it is not uncommon to find villages where the whole population had deteriorated in economic status between 1066 and 1086'. The severity and ruthlessness of the new big landlords and farmers unquestionably caused privation among the English peasantry and it was aggravated towards the end of the reign by poor harvests and bad weather.

On the other hand, an examination of the numbers of ploughs and ox teams recorded in the Domesday survey has been held to show that the peasantry was more prosperous than had previously been thought. It is possible, however, that these ploughs and teams were needed in order that the villagers could fulfil their obligations to their landlord by cultivating his

Norman soldiers foraging in the English countryside and rounding up sheep, cows and packhorses. The Saxon peasants suffered severely from the brutality of the Norman invaders who destroyed their property and pillaged their livestock and provisions.

estates two or three times a week. Those who believe that the peasants as a whole were no worse off at the end of the reign than they were at the beginning argue that the decline of the peasants, which otherwise appears to be clear from the Domesday records, was terminological rather than real. The commissioners, they say, were not interested in nice distinctions and their standards may have varied from circuit to circuit.

Two points have been stressed about the peasants in Norman England and their new masters. The first is that the differences between the Norman knight and the Saxon peasants (or *villani*) were greater than those between the Saxon thegn and the *ceorl* (or landholding peasant). Secondly, none of the Normans who came to England were themselves peasants – there was no mass immigration – or even expert agriculturalists. The conquerors came for what they could get and lived on the profits to be made out of their rents and dues. In spite of William's reiterated promises to uphold established customs, the rules of tenure were in fact tightened, even if the manorial superstructure was at first somewhat artificial. It may be that the peasants were less badly hit by the Norman Conquest than they were to become afterwards. Nevertheless the lowering of English peasant status had begun.

The great historian F. W. Maitland considered, largely though not entirely on the basis of evidence from Cambridgeshire, that the English peasantry was depressed after 1066; even those who maintain that little change took place in their economic situation in contrast with their legal status, admit that much distress was felt during William's reign, especially at its beginning and at its end. The harshness of the new landlords, the devastation of large parts of the kingdom, the building of castles at the expense of agricultural lands, and the enclosure of forest lands are undoubted facts, which, when added to the general impression conveyed at any rate superficially by both the Domesday survey and the *Anglo-Saxon Chronicle*, all point to the same conclusion – whatever qualifications are accepted – that the English peasants, like their former masters, were worse off as a result of the Norman Conquest.

8 The Achievement of William the Conqueror 1066-87

WHAT PLANS HAD WILLIAM in mind before he reached England in 1066? When he disembarked at Pevensey, he could scarcely have hoped that his victory over King Harold II would be so swift and so decisive. After all, it was easy enough to land in England, but to subdue it was more demanding. The King of Norway, who probably had nearly as large a force as William and the additional advantage of the alliance of the King of the Scots and of Harold's own brother Tostig, who had been influential in northern England, was soon beaten. It is likely that William was by no means sure that he would gain the crown; his Norman nobility had been pessimistic about his chances. No doubt what he intended to do if the battle was drawn or inconclusive was to offer to come to terms with King Harold, as he was later to do with the King of Denmark after the latter had successfully landed in England in 1070: thus William could have obtained money and booty and then withdrawn to Normandy.

As it was, the fact that Harold and his brothers were killed at Hastings meant that William was able to seize the throne. Clearly his original idea was to govern England in co-operation with the English aristocracy and to retain the framework of English law and customs. The destruction of the House of Godwin ensured that William had ample estates at his disposal with which to award the magnates who accompanied him from Normandy. However, when subsequently the Earls of Mercia and Northumbria conspired against him within three years of the Battle of Hastings, William abandoned this plan and instead he introduced or adapted Norman institutions and gradually handed over the government of the kingdom to Norman or French nobility.

The important point to realise is that however quickly William could move with his cavalry to suppress revolts, however easily warships could sail up and down the coast, England could not satisfactorily be controlled and governed without strong and dependable support in all parts of the kingdom. Edward the Confessor had earls or ealdormen and sheriffs as well as royal reeves. In later times, the monarchy was to rely on lords lieutenant and justices of the peace. It was not until the nineteenth century that improved communications made a centralised government really effective. What William did was to use the services of earls, whose domains were less extensive than those of Wessex, Mercia and Northumbria had been, in order to secure his kingdom against internal unrest or invasion from abroad. He would not allow any big shadows to menace his own authority as the House of Godwin had come to dominate the last years of Edward the Confessor's reign. William's earls were the precise equivalent of the *comtes* who served him in Normandy.

In the same way William upgraded the sheriffs: it was their duty to maintain justice and to collect taxes. Again, the sheriffs performed functions similar to those of the *vicomtes* in Normandy. When the King wanted to notify and enforce his own decisions, he relied upon the sheriffs to spread the news of them through the county courts; and if William wished to interfere with the course of justice, he sent his agents to the county courts to co-operate with the sheriffs. But in fact William made very few new laws; even the charter that he granted to the city of London confirming the customs that had prevailed there before was given in return for a supplication and was no doubt paid for. Moreover it did not really protect the city against further royal encroachments, as time was to prove. William was an administrator rather than a law-giver. The transformation that he wrought is England came principally through cultural, social and economic changes.

Before the Conquest, England was to some extent isolated from the cultural mainstream in Europe as a whole; the Normans, on the other hand, had, by the extension of their power to southern Italy and Sicily, promoted cultural contacts, particularly with the Moslem world. The Normans themselves were not originators but were cultural middlemen. The two able scholars who successively occupied the see of Canterbury under the Normans – Lanfranc and Anselm – were not in fact Normans. As a consequence of Norman rule, Latin and French became the two languages of the upper classes and they superseded the vernacular. Anglo-Saxon poetry and literature received a blow from which they took a long time to recover. It has also to be remembered that Anglo-Saxon sculpture, illumination of manuscripts and even church architecture were by no means negligible. But it is certainly arguable that, had it not been for the Normans, the twelfth-century renaissance might

The Art of Illumination

One of the first cultural achievements of the Anglo-Saxon period was the art of illumination, which flowered in the monastic centres of the country. The scribes who wrote and illustrated the bibles, psalters, and murals were held in the highest regard and worked under conditions of great strictness: they wrote in absolute silence, only the highest monastic officials were allowed to enter the scriptorium, and there was no artificial light for fear of fire. Books were written on vellum, a tough and lasting material whose only disadvantage was its high cost. With the coming of the Normans, illuminated manuscripts continued to be produced.

BELOW Initial 'C' from an eleventh-century manuscript, c. 1086, in the Durham style.

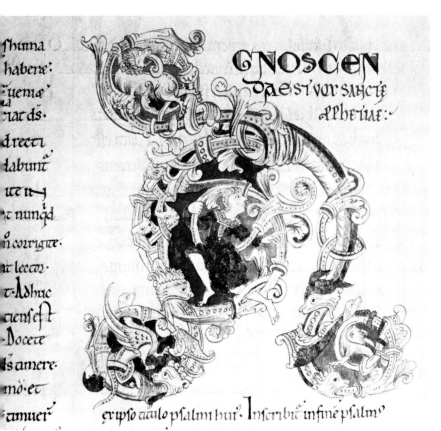

ABOVE The beginning of an eleventh-century St Mark's Gospel.

RIGHT Initial 'Q' from an eleventh-century manuscript written at Winchester c. 1600.

hpad

VID

puldpar

GLA

du

RIS

on yfelnerre

IN MALTA

þu þe   miltuʒ

QVI POENS

eaʃc   on   uu ʃuht ʃir

ES ININIQVI

neʃ   ʃe

TATE:

never have taken place. It was through Norman Italy that Greek erudition was transmitted to Latin Christendom. Presumably it would have reached England in any case, but it might have come there more slowly.

It was owing to Norman influence that historians began to write more fluently. Ordericus Vitalis, perhaps the most outstanding of these historians, was, it is true, born in England, but he did all his writing in a Norman monastery and it is to him that we owe so much admirably written information about the period. William of Poitiers, though not a historian of the same quality, attempted to harmonise the language of Virgil, Cicero and Caesar. Essentially he was a poet and indeed is said to have written poems, though they have not survived.

Apart from literature, the Normans stimulated architecture, especially church architecture. They did not of course introduce the Romanesque style with its familiar rounded arches into England. Even before the Conquest Edward the Confessor's Westminster Abbey was modelled on the Norman style. But most English churches built before the time of William were smaller than those built in Normandy. The churches put up by the Normans had longer naves and elaborate Lady chapels. Nevertheless, Professor Douglas tells us, the development of architecture in England during William's reign owed more to the Norman rulers than the Norman artists. We are told that Aldred, the Archbishop of York, who visited Germany, preferred a Teutonic to a Romanesque style and introduced at Beverley a screen 'skilfully fashioned of Teutonic work'. Undoubtedly the Normans made a profound impression on church architecture, employing English craftsmen to build and extend cathedrals and abbeys. Sculpture, as well as architecture, was stimulated by the Normans, although whether one prefers the Norman to the Anglo-Saxon style of building and sculpting must be a matter of individual taste.

To turn to the political results of the Norman Conquest, William undoubtedly conferred strong government upon England. To put it bluntly, he was an autocrat, though he found it harder to enforce his authority in England than in Normandy. Under Edward the Confessor, it has been said, the kingdom was weakly ruled. Edward was not an energetic or loquacious king. Half his dominions he never even visited. The earls of Wessex, Mercia and Northumbria all governed vast areas in which they were semi-independent. Except during the crisis of 1051, Edward preferred tact and diplomacy to curbing his nobility by a threat of force. King William, for his part, split up the ancient English earldoms and confided local government to men whom he trusted and over whom he exercised tight control. The establishment of border earldoms and the distribution of royal castles throughout the land ensured – or should have ensured – both internal and external security. In fact, the extreme north of the kingdom was never satisfactorily organised during William's reign and the northern counties were omitted from the Domesday survey. Their very sovereignty was still disputed by the Scots. Elsewhere, using both the powers that had been possessed by the Anglo-Saxon monarchs and the methods of administration that had proved effective in Normandy, William (it has been maintained) was able to impose political unity and good order.

It was of course to the interest of the conquerors to guard and preserve their newly-found wealth. The corporate fine that was imposed upon the hundreds if a Norman were murdered was typical of the way in which William looked after his own. Under his government, wrote Ordericus Vitalis, 'the native inhabitants were crushed, imprisoned, disinherited, banished and scattered beyond the limits of their own country; while his own vassals and adherents were exalted to wealth and honours and raised to all offices of state'. The English language was reduced to an inferior position and the status of many English peasants declined. It may be argued that they were no worse off economically than they had been before, but the fact remains that the freemen and 'sokemen' began to lose their privileges and the long process by which the villagers became serfs subject to all sorts of burdens imposed upon them by manorial lords had started. Moreover, the Normans and other Frenchmen who replaced the English as the principal landowners were little concerned with agriculture *per se*; they loved fighting and hunting and hawking; they preferred to exploit their landed property by handing it over to the mercies of farmers or bailiffs in order to extract as large rents as they could out of it. 'It was,' writes Frank Barlow, 'a restless, drunken and emotional society, gorged after 1066 with unaccustomed wealth.' Nor, perhaps,

'The native inhabitants were crushed'

Iste Wills dõi Bastardus dux Normanos anghani sibi expulso Rege
Haraldo triumphator magnificus potent Adquisita sub iugu
Abbacia de bello ubi triumphat fundau. Regnau anis xvi. 7 aplus

Iste Wills Rufus dictus 7 existens anglos nobiles quix p̄
rem ei receperit vipm equere micipis fatigau 7 expulii
Aula Westm̃ ostruit. Tande sagita puc ipm regnauit am
cim̃

Willelm̄ Rex
anglie pñi pc̃o
quisic onem ei

Willelm̄
Rex sec̄
Rufus

Henricus se
nior Rex tci.
cm̃ — xv — cm̃

Stephã
Rex tc̃
cccc

Iste henricus vir potens 7 sapiens iurau leges sci edmardi iui
adustit tene. s; ipm uicar frem suu noluit. Nobile cenobiu de
Radingo ubi sepult iac; fundau 7 epati ostruit Rex F. Regnau au
trinis xxxvi. 7 tciter dimidiu. cm̃ — xxxv — cm̃

Iste Stephanus miles strenuissim̃ onib; dieb;
dubus castl; bellouar siout̃ abbaciam de feuresham
fundauit. In qua ipe 7 vstac fili eius 7 mahildis regi
uxor ei iacent sepult. Iste Regnauit annis xix.

were the Normans notably efficient or adventurous in their ideas. Dr Richardson and Professor Sayles are of the opinion that the Normans 'had little statesmanship and little foresight', that 'they were barbarians who were becoming conscious of their insufficiency'. That is a severe judgment. At any rate, they introduced measures radical enough to transform the operation of English government and to alter drastically the island's way of life. But it can be'maintained that they conquered a people at least as civilised – and possibly more civilised – than themselves. Perhaps the seventeenth-century Levellers were not so wrong when they complained of 'the Norman yoke'.

Whatever may have happened later in the development of the 'Anglo-Norman state', the English were forced to recognise that they were a subjected people who had to pay the penalty for the defeat of Harold II at the Battle of Hastings. 'It was', writes Professor Loyn, 'a harsh world that these Normans introduced for all the brilliance and glitter.' He stresses that not only the status of peasants but that of women declined. The Normans, being a race of warriors, put an end to the conditions of rough equality which had existed between men and women in Anglo-Saxon times. Under the Normans, the inferior position of women, inculcated by St Paul, was accepted without question. A woman passed from the subjection of her father to that of her husband about whom she had small choice. She acquired some measure of independence only if she became a wealthy widow.

To the Normans England was a ripe fruit which had fallen almost unexpectedly into their hands. As John Le Patourel has observed, 'the Normans not only exploited England to fulfil their wider ambitions, they exploited it for the direct enrich-ment of Normandy'. The twin abbeys at Caen were largely paid for out of English money and so were the extensions to the cathedral of Bayeux. William the Conqueror and a handful of magnates who were related to him are estimated to have owned almost half the lands of England. The Normans obtained be-sides lands and money the services of Englishmen to fight in their Continental wars. In return what did they have to offer? A monastic revival? An architectural renaissance? Economic expansion or agricultural improvements? An outstandingly efficient system of government? If so, it did not last for very

209

Medieval Craftsmanship

RIGHT Anglo-Saxon paving stone found at St Paul's, dated *c.* 1030.

BELOW The raising of Lazarus, one of a pair of carved stone panels in the south aisle of the choir at Chichester Cathedral. Authorities differ about whether they are Anglo-Saxon work of the early eleventh century, or Norman work *c.* 1130. The sculptures show a rare intensity of feeling and are among the best surviving works of this period in England.

BELOW Carved capital from the crypt of Canterbury Cathedral, one of a series of richly carved capitals of the highest artistic quality. They appear to date from the 1120s and the subjects are drawn from fable: curious animals and fantastic monsters, some of them apparently of Eastern origin.

RIGHT ABOVE AND BELOW Twelfth-century carvings from the late Romanesque church of St Mary and St David at Kilpeck. The glory of the church is its rich sculptural decoration, which show a variety of influences: Celtic, Scandinavian and western French.

long. It has not been conclusively proved that any class of Englishmen was materially better off, even in the long run, as a result of the Conquest.

But it has sometimes been argued that to think of William's achievements in terms of the debasement of the English is an anachronistic mistake. An instance of this point of view has been taken from the *Divi Britannici*, which was written by Sir Winston Churchill, the father of the first Duke of Marlborough, and originally published in 1675. Churchill paid a tribute to those who fought against King William saying 'they were made immortal who bravely strove with Destiny to save their country from the calamity of foreign servitude'. But the resistance by King Harold, it is contended, was in fact no national struggle: it was 'a triangular contest between a Norman Duke, a Norwegian King and a West Saxon Earl'. Yet it is surely legitimate to compare the situation of the kingdom of England as it was under Edward the Confessor with what it was to become under William the Norman.

Edward, as has already been pointed out, was neither such an energetic administrator as William nor so vigorous a soldier. His motto might even have been *quieta non movere* (let sleeping dogs lie) as it was that of Sir Robert Walpole and Stanley Baldwin. The *Anglo-Saxon Chronicle* asserts that the land tax or geld ceased to be collected by Edward after 1051; in any case, taxation was less onerous than after the Conquest. Edward was not an extravagant king and he had no children to provide for. His only indulgence was the building of Westminster Abbey; he lived on the revenues of his own lands and did not alienate those of his subjects. His income is estimated to have been £5,500 a year as compared with William's £11,000 a year. Little of the wealth of the kingdom was then diverted into unproductive enterprises such as the building of castles. Edward was both less extravagant and less greedy than William the Conqueror.

During the last fifteen years of the reign of Edward the Confessor, not only was England at peace but the climate was becoming milder and population rising. 'The increased demand for food,' writes Professor Barlow, 'encouraged improvements in agricultural techniques and inevitably it favoured arable as against pastoral farming. More land went under the plough.'

212

Growing prosperity profited landlords who invested capital in extending farm buildings and endowing churches. Edward's avowed aim was to protect his subjects and to advance his kingdom 'in the quietness of peace'. The Anglo-Saxon courts were popular assemblies in which rights as well as duties were enforced; and the judicial system – unlike the complicated and conflicting jurisdictions in William's reign – was a unified one. According to the contemporary *Life of King Edward*, which is admittedly flattering, he appointed good justices and enacted good laws. The Anglo-Saxon Chronicler wrote that he 'protected his fatherland, his realm and his people'. Moreover, he overcame difficulties on his borders. King Gruffydd ap Llywelyn of Wales and King Malcolm III of Scots acknowledged that they were his vassals, but he did not attempt to interfere in Wales or Scotland or to exact tribute from them. It was only when Gruffydd, who had been accepted as king of the whole of Wales in 1055, attempted to thrust his influence eastward into Herefordshire that Edward was compelled to take action against him and, with the aid of Earl Harold of Wessex, defeated him and obliged the Welsh princes to promise to be faithful vassals. Broadly, the kingdom of England was more politically and militarily secure than Normandy if only because it was an island, while the frontiers of Normandy were not at all easily defensible and consequently were a continual source of unsettlement, rebellion and conflict.

If, then, the reign of William the Conqueror and the coming of the Normans are considered in the light of the reign of Edward the Confessor, it is difficult to see that the kingdom of England was materially better off either in the short run or in the long run. For hundreds of years the resources of a fertile and prospering land were to be diverted to fulfil impossible political ambitions on the other side of the Channel. It was to be hundreds of years also, after the English peasantry had been reduced to a state of serfdom, before they obtained complete emancipation from feudal subjection to their manorial lords. Naturally the contrast between the two reigns must not be exaggerated. While it is true that William's devastation of the Midlands and the north of England created distress and famine, the scars of which remained until almost the end of the reign, probably the tillers of the soil as a whole were economically not greatly

'Protected his fatherland, his realm and his people'

213

ABOVE Seal of William
the Conqueror.

RIGHT Edward the
Confessor at a banquet,
from a fourteenth-century
manuscript.

worse off than they had been before. The structure of the county
courts and hundred courts stayed intact and it is possible that
the suitors at these courts hardly noticed the change in their
masters. Indeed it has been maintained that for half a century
after 1066 the English way of life 'was not sensibly altered'.
Both Edward and William intervened from time to time in the
running of the county courts: they represented, as it were, a
dispersal of the King's own Court, for they were supervised by
men whom the kings trusted. William did not change the
traditional English laws and customs; what he did was to add
to them and confuse them. The idea that he deliberately introduced an entirely novel and uniform method of government

can no longer be accepted. He was, as it were, the passive agent of revolutionary changes. But he was in no way an original thinker nor did he possess the gift, which is the mark of great statesmanship, of being able to plan for the future instead of simply solving day-to-day problems as they arose. A recent assessment of his work by the two British historians already quoted is that 'he seems to have been astute without wisdom, resolute without foresight, a man of very limited aims and very limited vision, narrow, ignorant and superstitious'.

Finally one must recognise that the concept of a tidy 'feudal system', which was invented by seventeenth-century lawyers and antiquarians, and was investigated with impressive scholarship by Victorian historians who soaked themselves in Domesday Book, is untenable. The essential fact about the reign of William the Conqueror is, as has been emphasised throughout this book, that a foreign aristocracy or plutocracy was superimposed as the governing class in England. It introduced a somewhat wider culture, but it contributed little to the happiness of the bulk of King William's subjects: the conquest was achieved at a terrible cost out of all proportion to the benefits that it conferred. It is not unfair to recall what William is supposed to have said when he was dying:

> I persecuted the native inhabitants of England beyond all reason. Whether nobles or commons, I cruelly oppressed them; many I unjustly disinherited; innumerable multitudes, especially in the county of York, perished through me by famine and sword . . . I am stained with the rivers of blood that I have shed.

Chronology

1028	William the Conqueror is born.
1035	He succeeds his father as Duke of Normandy.
1047	He begins to establish his authority, with the aid of his overlord, King Henry I of France, by defeating Guy of Burgundy, who seeks to become Duke of Normandy, at the Battle of Val-ès-Dunes.
1051	He marries Matilda, daughter of Count Baldwin V of Flanders.
1064	He is visited by Harold, Earl of Wessex.
1066	(28 September) He lands at Pevensey and (14 October) wins the Battle of Hastings. (25 December) He is crowned in Westminster Abbey.
1069–70	William devastates the north of England and part of the Midlands after invasion by the King of Denmark.
1071	English resistance to the Normans is suppressed.
1072	William invades Scotland and concludes Treaty of Abernethy with King Malcolm III.
1075	He suppresses revolt of three earls.
1079	(January) William is defeated by his eldest son Robert Curthose, at the Battle of Gerberoy (near Beauvais).
1080	William rejects request by Pope Gregory VII for an oath of fealty.
1082	He imprisons his half-brother Odo, Bishop of Bayeux and Earl of Kent, who aspires to become Pope.
1083	(2 November) Death of his wife, Queen Matilda.
1085	(Christmas) William plans 'Domesday' survey.
1086	(August) He meets his tenants-in-chief and other lords at Salisbury and obtains oath of fealty.
1087	(9 September) William dies at priory of Saint Gervais outside Rouen and is buried at Caen.

Genealogical tree

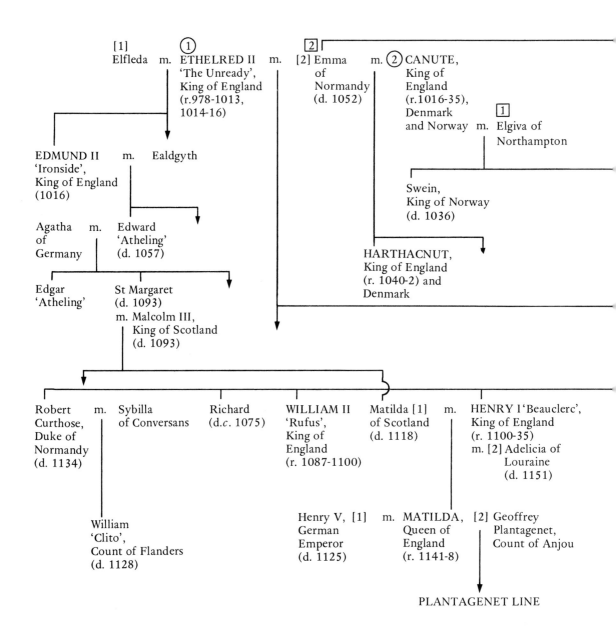

[1] Elfleda m. ① ETHELRED II m. [2] Emma m. ② CANUTE,
'The Unready', of King of
King of England Normandy England
(r.978-1013, (d. 1052) (r.1016-35),
1014-16) Denmark
and Norway m. Elgiva of [1]
Northampton

EDMUND II m. Ealdgyth
'Ironside',
King of England
(1016)

Swein,
King of Norway
(d. 1036)

Agatha m. Edward
of 'Atheling'
Germany (d. 1057)

HARTHACNUT,
King of England
(r. 1040-2) and
Denmark

Edgar St Margaret
'Atheling' (d. 1093)
m. Malcolm III,
King of Scotland
(d. 1093)

Robert m. Sybilla Richard WILLIAM II Matilda [1] m. HENRY I 'Beauclerc',
Curthose, of Conversans (d.c. 1075) 'Rufus', of Scotland King of England
Duke of King of (d. 1118) (r. 1100-35)
Normandy England m. [2] Adelicia of
(d. 1134) (r. 1087-1100) Louraine
(d. 1151)

William
'Clito',
Count of Flanders
(d. 1128)

Henry V, [1] m. MATILDA, [2] Geoffrey
German Queen of Plantagenet,
Emperor England Count of Anjou
(d. 1125) (r. 1141-8)

PLANTAGENET LINE

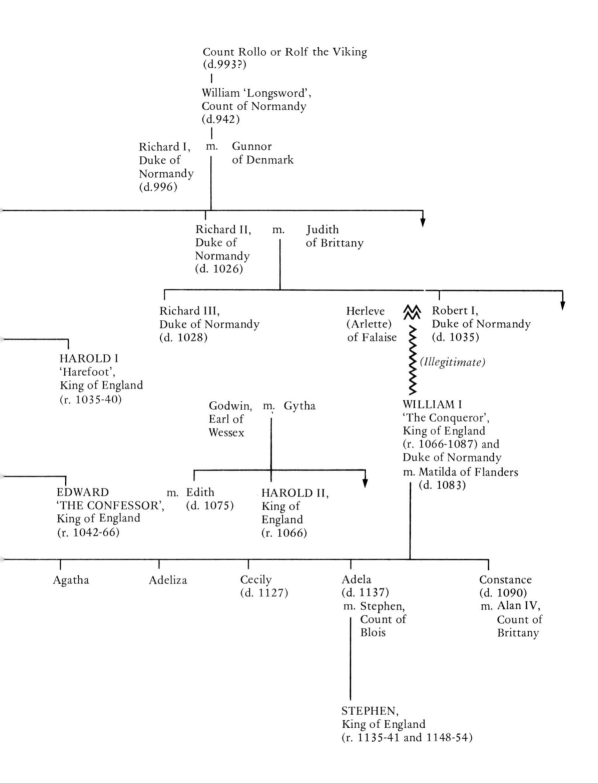

Count Rollo or Rolf the Viking
(d.993?)

William 'Longsword',
Count of Normandy
(d.942)

Richard I, m. Gunnor
Duke of   of Denmark
Normandy
(d.996)

Richard II, m. Judith
Duke of   of Brittany
Normandy
(d. 1026)

Richard III,
Duke of Normandy
(d. 1028)

Herleve
(Arlette)
of Falaise

Robert I,
Duke of Normandy
(d. 1035)

(Illegitimate)

HAROLD I
'Harefoot',
King of England
(r. 1035-40)

Godwin, m. Gytha
Earl of
Wessex

WILLIAM I
'The Conqueror',
King of England
(r. 1066-1087) and
Duke of Normandy
m. Matilda of Flanders
(d. 1083)

EDWARD   m. Edith
'THE CONFESSOR',   (d. 1075)
King of England
(r. 1042-66)

HAROLD II,
King of
England
(r. 1066)

Agatha

Adeliza

Cecily
(d. 1127)

Adela
(d. 1137)
m. Stephen,
Count of
Blois

Constance
(d. 1090)
m. Alan IV,
Count of
Brittany

STEPHEN,
King of England
(r. 1135-41 and 1148-54)

Select bibliography

PRIMARY AUTHORITIES

The Anglo-Saxon Chronicle, trans. G. N. Garmonsway (new ed., 1990)

The Bayeux Tapestry (Thames & Hudson, 1985)

The Carmen de Hastingae Proelio, ed. Catherine Morton and Hope Muntz (1972)

English Historical Documents 1042–1159, ed. D. C. Douglas and G. W. Greenaway (1953) (This contains extracts from William of Jumiège's *Gesta* and the writing of the so-called Monk of Caen)

Histoire de Guillaume le Conquérant by Guillaume de Poitiers, ed. and trans. Raymonde Foreville (Paris, 1952)

The Ecclesiastical History of England and Normandy by Ordericus Vitalis, trans. Thomas Forester (1856) and ed. and trans. Marjorie Chibnall (1969, 1972)

The Laws of English Kings from Edward to Henry I, ed. A. J. Robertson (1925)

SECONDARY AUTHORITIES

E. S. Armitage, *Early Norman Castles in the British Isles* (1912)

Frank Barlow, *William I and the Norman Conquest* (1965)
   Edward the Confessor (1970)
   The Feudal Kingdom of England 1042–1216 (rev. ed. 1972)

David Bates, *William the Conqueror* (1989)

Christopher Brooke, *The Saxon and Norman Kings* (1967)

Z. N. Brooke, *The English Church and the Papacy* (1931)

R. Allen Brown, *The Norman Conquest* (1984)
   William the Conqueror and the Battle of Hastings (1988)

A. W. Clapham, *English Romanesque Architecture after the Conquest* (1934)

Charles W. David, *Robert Curthose, Duke of Normandy* (1920)

David C. Douglas, *William the Conqueror* (1964)
   The Norman Achievement (1969)

E. A. Freeman, *The History of the Norman Conquest of England*, 6 vols (1870–9)

V. H. Galbraith, *The Making of Domesday Book* (1961)

Elizabeth M. Hallam, *Domesday Book through Nine Centuries* (1986)

C. Warren Hollister, *The Military Organization of Norman England* (1965)

David Howarth, *The Year of the Conquest* (1977)

S. Körner, *The Battle of Hastings, England and Europe* (1964)

R. V. Lennard, *Rural England 1086–1135* (1959)

H. R. Loyn, *Anglo-Saxon England and the Norman Conquest* (1970)
The Norman Conquest (1982)

A. J. Macdonald, *Lanfranc* (1944)

D. F. Renn, *Norman Castles in Britain* (1968)

H. G. Richardson and G. O. Sayles, *The Governance of Medieval England from the Conquest to Magna Carta* (1963)

R. L. G. Ritchie, *The Normans and Scotland* (1954)

Trevor Rowley, *The Norman Heritage 1066–1200* (1983)

Peter Sawyer (ed.), *Domesday Book: A Reassessment* (1987)

Doris M. Stenton, *English Justice 1066–1215* (1964)
English Society in the Early Middle Ages 1066–1307 (4th ed., 1965)

F. M. Stenton, *William the Conqueror and the Rule of the Normans* (1908)
Anglo-Saxon England (3rd ed., 1971)

Paul Zumthor, *Guillaume le Conquérant* (1964)

LECTURES, ARTICLES AND PAMPHLETS

Frank Barlow, *Edward the Confessor and the Norman Conquest* (English Historical Association, 1971)

David C. Douglas, 'The Norman Conquest and English Feudalism' (*Economic History Review*, 1939)
'Companions of the Conqueror' (*History*, 1943)
The Norman Conquest and British Historians (Glasgow, 1946)
'Edward the Confessor, Duke William of Normandy and the English Succession' (*English Historical Review*, 1953)
'The Bishops of Normandy 1035–1066' (*Cambridge Historical Journal*, 1957)

Richard Glover, 'English Warfare in 1066' (*English Historical Review*, 1952)

J. C. Holt, 'Feudalism Revisited' (*English Historical Review*, 1961–2)

T. J. Oleson, 'Edward the Confessor's Promise of the Throne to Duke William of Normandy' (*English Historical Review*, 1953)

John Le Patourel, *Normandy and England 1066–1144* (University of Reading, 1971)

J. O. Prestwich, 'War and Finance in the Anglo-Norman State' (*Transactions of the Royal Historical Society*, 1953)
'Anglo-Norman Feudalism and the Problem of Continuity' (*Past and Present*, 1963)

Index